SECOND EDITION

# Python
## *Pocket Reference*

*Mark Lutz*

Beijing · Cambridge · Farnham · Köln · Paris · Sebastopol · Taipei · Tokyo

**Python Pocket Reference, Second Edition**
by Mark Lutz

Published by O'Reilly & Associates, Inc., 1005 Gravenstein Highway
North, Sebastopol, CA 95472.

O'Reilly & Associates books may be purchased for educational,
business, or sales promotional use. Online editions are also available for
most titles (*safari.oreilly.com*). For more information contact our
corporate/institutional sales department: 800-998-9938 or
*corporate@oreilly.com*.

| | |
|---|---|
| **Editor:** | Laura Lewin |
| **Production Editor:** | Rachel Wheeler |
| **Cover Designer:** | Edie Freedman |
| **Interior Designer:** | David Futato |

**Printing History:**

| | |
|---|---|
| October 1998: | First Edition. |
| January 2002: | Second Edition. |

0-596-00189-4
[C]                                                              [3/02]

# Contents

# Python Pocket Reference

## Introduction

Python is a general-purpose, object-oriented, and open source computer programming language. It is commonly used for both standalone programs and scripting applications in a wide variety of domains, by hundreds of thousands of developers.

Python is designed to optimize developer productivity, software quality, program portability, and component integration. Python programs run on most platforms in common use, including mainframes and supercomputers, Unix and Linux, Windows and Macintosh, Palm OS and WinCE, Java and .NET, and more.

This pocket reference summarizes Python statements and types, built-in functions, commonly used library modules, and other prominent Python tools. It is intended to serve as a concise reference tool for developers and is designed to be a companion to other books that provide tutorials, code examples, and other learning materials.

This second edition covers Python Release 2.2 and later. It has been thoroughly updated for recent language and library changes and expanded for new topics. Most of it applies to earlier releases as well, with the exception of recent language extensions.

# Conventions

[ ]   Something in brackets is usually optional.

*     Something followed by an asterisk can be repeated zero
      or more times.

*a | b*
      Items separated by a bar are often alternatives.

*italic*
      Used for filenames and URLs and to highlight new terms.

`constant width`
      Used for code, commands, and command-line options,
      and to indicate the names of modules, functions,
      attributes, etc.

`constant width italic`
      Used for replaceable parameter names in command
      syntax.

# Command-Line Options

```
python [option*]
   [ scriptfilename | -c command | - ] [arg*]
```

## Python Options

-d   Turn on parser debugging output (for developers of the
     Python core).

-i   Enter interactive mode after executing a script or com-
     mand, without reading the PYTHONSTARTUP file. Use-
     ful for postmortem debugging.

-O   Optimize generated byte-code (create and use *.pyo* byte-
     code files). Currently yields a minor performance
     improvement.

-OO  Like -O, but also removes docstrings from byte-code.

-S  Don't imply "import site" on initialization.

-t  Issue warnings about inconsistent tab usage (-tt issues error instead).

-u  Force stdout and stderr to be unbuffered and binary.

-U  Unicode literals: 'xxx' treated like u'xxx' (highly experimental in 2.1.1).

-v  Print a message each time a module is initialized, showing the place from which it is loaded; repeat this flag for more verbose output.

-x  Skip first line of source, allowing use of non-Unix forms of #!cmd.

-h  Print help message and exit.

-V  Print Python version number and exit.

-W *arg*
    Warning control; arg is *action*:*message*:*category*:*module*: *lineno*. See warnings module documentation, new in 2.1, in the Python Library Reference (*http://www.python.org/doc/*).

## Program Specification

*scriptfilename*
    The name of a Python scriptfile to execute; the main, topmost file of a program, made available in sys.argv[0].

-c *command*
    Specifies a Python command (as a string) to execute; sys.argv[0] is set to -c.

-   Read Python commands from stdin (the default); enter interactive mode if stdin is a tty.

*arg**
    Anything else on the command line is passed to the scriptfile or command (and appears in the built-in list of strings sys.argv[1:]).

If no *scriptfilename* or *command* is given, Python enters inter-active mode, reading commands from stdin (and uses GNU readline, if installed, for input).

Besides traditional command lines, Python programs can also generally be started by clicking on their filenames in a file explorer GUI, by calling functions in the Python/C API, by using program launch menu options in IDEs such as IDLE and Komodo, and so on.

# Environment Variables

*PYTHONPATH*
> Augments the default search path for module files. The format is the same as the shell's PATH setting: directory pathnames separated by colons (semicolons on DOS). On module imports, Python searches for the corresponding file in each listed directory, from left to right. Merged into sys.path.

*PYTHONSTARTUP*
> If set to the name of a readable file, the Python com-mands in that file are executed before the first prompt is displayed in interactive mode.

*PYTHONHOME*
> If set, the value is used as an alternate prefix directory for library modules (or sys.prefix, sys.exec_prefix). The default module search path uses sys.prefix/lib.

*PYTHONCASEOK*
> If set, ignore case in import statements (Windows, new in 2.1).

*PYTHONDEBUG*
> If nonempty, same as -d option.

*PYTHONINSPECT*
> If nonempty, same as -i option.

*PYTHONOPTIMIZE*
    If nonempty, same as -O option.

*PYTHONUNBUFFERED*
    If nonempty, same as -u option.

*PYTHONVERBOSE*
    If nonempty, same as -v option.

# Built-in Types and Operators

## Operators and Precedence

Table 1 lists Python's expression operators. Operators in the lower cells of this table have higher precedence (i.e., bind tighter) when used in mixed-operator expressions without parentheses.

*Table 1. Expression operators and precedence*

| Operators | Description |
| --- | --- |
| `lambda args: expr` | Anonymous function maker |
| `X or Y` | Logical OR: Y is evaluated only if X is false |
| `X and Y` | Logical AND: Y is evaluated only if X is true |
| `not X` | Logical negation |
| `X < Y, X <= Y, X > Y,`<br>`X >= Y, X == Y, X <> Y,`<br>`X != Y, X is Y, X is not Y,`<br>`X in S, X not in S` | Comparison operators,[a] equality operators, inequality operators, object identity tests, sequence membership |
| `X \| Y` | Bitwise OR |
| `X ^ Y` | Bitwise exclusive OR |
| `X & Y` | Bitwise AND |
| `X << Y, X >> Y` | Shift X left, right by Y bits |
| `X + Y, X - Y` | Addition/concatenation, subtraction |
| `X * Y, X % Y,`<br>`X / Y, X // Y` | Multiply/repetition, remainder/format, division, floor division[b] |

*Table 1. Expression operators and precedence (continued)*

| Operators | Description |
|---|---|
| -X, +X, ~X, X**Y | Unary negation, identity, bitwise complement, power |
| X[i], X[i:j], X.attr, X(...) | Indexing, slicing, attribute references, function calls |
| (...), [...], {...}, `...` | Tuple, list,[c] dictionary, conversion to string[d] |

[a] Comparison operators may be chained: x < y < z is similar to x < y  and y < z, except that y is evaluated only once in the first format.

[b] *Floor* division (X // Y), new in 2.2, always truncates fractional remainders. *Classic* division (X / Y) truncates integer division results in 2.2 but will be changed to *true* division (always keeping remainders) in 3.0. In 2.2, use from __future__ import true_division to make the / operator return true division result (e.g., 1/2 is 0.5).

[c] List literals in square brackets ([ ... ]) may be a simple list of expressions, or a *list comprehension*; see "Lists" in the section "Specific Built-in Types."

[d] String conversion expressions are equivalent to calling the built-in repr function; the built-in str function provides an alternative conversion.

## Operations by Category

All built-in types support the comparisons and Boolean operations listed in Table 2.

Boolean *true* means any nonzero number or any nonempty collection object (list, dictionary, etc.). The special object None is false.

Comparisons return 1 or 0 and are applied recursively in compound objects as needed to determine a result.

Boolean and and or operators stop as soon as a result is known (short-circuit) and return one of the two operand objects (on left or right).

*Table 2. Comparisons and Boolean operations*

| Operator | Description |
|---|---|
| X < Y | Strictly less than[a] |
| X <= Y | Less than or equal |
| X > Y | Strictly greater than |
| X >= Y | Greater than or equal |

*Table 2. Comparisons and Boolean operations (continued)*

| Operator | Description |
|---|---|
| X == Y | Equal (same value) |
| X != Y | Not equal (same as X< >Y)[b] |
| X is Y | Same object |
| X is not Y | Negated object identity |
| X < Y < Z | Chained comparisons |
| not X | If X is false then 1, else 0 |
| X or Y | If X is false then Y; else, X |
| X and Y | If X is false then X; else, Y |

[a] For comparison expression overloading, see both the rich comparison (e.g., __lt__ for <) and general __cmp__ class methods in the section "Operator Overloading Methods."

[b] != and <> both mean not equal by value, but != is the preferred syntax. is performs identity test; == performs value comparison.

Tables 3 through 6 define operations common to types in the three major type categories (sequence, mapping, and number), as well as operations available for mutable (changeable) types in Python. Most types also export additional type-specific operations (e.g., methods), as described in the later section "Specific Built-in Types."

*Table 3. Sequence operations (strings, lists, tuples)*

| Operation | Description | Class method |
|---|---|---|
| X in S,<br>X not in S | Membership tests | __contains__,<br>__getitem__ |
| for X in S: | Iteration | __getitem__,<br>__iter__ [a] |
| S + S | Concatenation | __add__ |
| S * N, N * S | Repetition | __mul__ |
| S[i] | Index by offset | __getitem__ |
| S[i:j] | Slicing | __getslice__,[b]<br>__getitem__ |
| len(S) | Length | __len__ |
| iter(S) | Iterator object | __iter__ |

*Table 3. Sequence operations (strings, lists, tuples) (continued)*

| Operation | Description | Class method |
|-----------|-------------|--------------|
| min(S) | Minimum item | __getitem__ |
| max(S) | Maximum item | __getitem__ |

a  See also Python 2.2 iterators, generators, and __iter__ class method (see "The yield Statement" in "Specific Statements"). If defined, __contains__ is preferred over __iter__, and __iter__ is preferred over __getitem__.
b  Since 2.0, __getslice__, __setslice__, and __delslice__ have been somewhat deprecated in favor of passing slice objects to their item-based counterparts; see the section "Operator Overloading Methods."

*Table 4. Mutable sequence operations (lists)*

| Operation | Description | Class method |
|-----------|-------------|--------------|
| S[i] = X | Index assignment: change item at existing offset i | __setitem__ |
| S[i:j] = S | Slice assignment | __setslice__, __setitem__ |
| del S[i] | Index deletion | __delitem__ |
| del S[i:j] | Slice deletion | __delslice__, __delitem__ |

*Table 5. Mapping operations (dictionaries)*

| Operation | Description | Class method |
|-----------|-------------|--------------|
| D[k] | Index by key | __getitem__ |
| D[k] = X | Key assignment: change or create entry for key k | __setitem__ |
| del D[k] | Delete item by key | __delitem__ |
| len(D) | Length (number of keys) | __len__ |

*Table 6. Numeric operations (all number types)*

| Operation | Description | Class method |
|-----------|-------------|--------------|
| X + Y, X – Y | Add, subtract | __add__, __sub__ |
| X * Y, X / Y, X % Y | Multiply, divide, remainder | __mul__, __div__, __mod__ |
| -X, +X | Negative, identity | __neg__, __pos__ |

*Table 6. Numeric operations (all number types) (continued)*

| Operation | Description | Class method |
|---|---|---|
| X \| Y, X & Y, X ^ Y | Bitwise OR, AND, exclusive OR (integers) | __or__, __and__, __xor__ |
| X << N, X >> N | Bitwise left-shift, right-shift (integers) | __lshift__, __rshift__ |
| ~X | Bitwise invert (integers) | __invert__ |
| X ** Y | X to the power Y | __pow__ |
| abs(X) | Absolute value | __abs__ |
| int(X) | Convert to integer | __int__ |
| long(X) | Convert to long | __long__ |
| float(X) | Convert to float | __float__ |
| complex(X), complex(re,im) | Make a complex | __complex__ |
| divmod(X, Y) | Tuple: (X/Y, X%Y) | __divmod__ |
| pow(X, Y [,Z]) | Raise to a power | __pow__ |

## Sequence Operation Notes

### Indexing: S[i]

- Fetches components at offsets (first item is at offset 0).
- Negative indexes means count backward from the end.
- S[0] fetches the first item.
- S[-2] fetches the second from the end (S[len(S) - 2]).

### Slicing: S[i:j]

- Extracts contiguous sections of a sequence.
- Slice boundaries default to 0 and sequence length.
- S[1:3] fetches from offsets 1 up to but not including 3.
- S[1:] fetches from offsets 1 through the end (length–1).
- S[:-1] fetches from offsets 0 up to but not including the last item.

- S[:] makes a top-level copy of sequence object S.
- Slice assignment is like deleting and then inserting.

**Other**

- Concatenation, repetition, and slicing return new objects.

# Specific Built-in Types

This section covers numbers, strings, lists, dictionaries, tuples, and files. Compound data types (e.g., lists, dictionaries, tuples) can nest inside each other arbitrarily.

## Numbers

This section covers basic number types (integers, floating-point), as well as more advanced types (complex, unlimited-precision long integers).

### Constants

Numbers are written in a variety of numeric constant forms:

1234, -24, 0
  Normal integers (C longs, at least 32 bits)

99999999L, 42l
  Long integers (unlimited size)

1.23, 3.14e-10, 4E210, 4.0e+210
  Floating-point (C doubles)

0177, 0x9ff
  Octal and hex integer constants

3+4j, 3.0+4.0j, 3J
  Complex numbers

### Operations

Number types support all number operations (see Table 6). In mixed-type expressions, Python converts operands up to the type of the "highest" type, where integer is lower than long, which is lower than floating-point, which is lower than complex.

In 2.2, integer operations are automatically promoted to longs instead of overflowing, and there are two flavors of division (/ and //).

# Strings

Strings are immutable (unchangeable) arrays of characters, accessed by offset.

## Constants

Strings are written as a series of characters in quotes:

`"Python's", 'Python"s'`
> Double and single quotes work the same, and each can embed unescaped quotes of the other kind.

```
"""This is a
multiline block"""
```
> Triple-quoted blocks collect lines into a single string, with end-of-line markers between the original lines.

`'Python\'s\n'`
> Backslash escape code sequences (see Table 7) are replaced with the special-character byte values they represent (e.g., '\n' is a byte with binary value 012).

`"This" "is" "concatenated"`
> Adjacent string constants are concatenated.

`r'a raw\string', R'another\one'`
> Raw strings: backslashes are retained literally (handy for regular expressions and DOS directory paths; e.g., r'c:\dir1\file').

`u"..."`
> Unicode string constants (see "Unicode strings" later in this section).

*Table 7. String constant escape codes*

| Escape | Meaning | Escape | Meaning |
|--------|---------|--------|---------|
| \newline | Ignored continuation | \t | Horizontal tab |
| \\ | Backslash (\) | \v | Vertical tab |
| \' | Single quote (') | \N{id} | Unicode dbase id |
| \" | Double quote (") | \uhhhh | Unicode 16-bit hex |
| \a | Bell | \Uhhhh... | Unicode 32-bit hex[a] |
| \b | Backspace | \xhh | Hex digits value |
| \f | Formfeed | \ooo | Octal digits value |
| \n | Linefeed | \0 | Null (not end string) |
| \r | Carriage return | \other | Not an escape |

[a] \Uhhhh... takes exactly eight hexadecimal digits (h); both \u and \U can be used only in Unicode string constants.

## Operations

All sequence operations (shown earlier in Table 3), plus %
string formatting expressions, plus string method calls (see
"String methods"). String formatting replaces % targets on the
left with values on the right (similar to C's sprintf).

```
"The knights who say %s!" % "Ni!"
```
Result: "The knights who say Ni!"

```
"%d %s %d you" % (1, 'spam', 4.0)
```
Result: "1 spam 4 you"

```
"%(n)d %(x)s" % {"n":1, "x":"spam"}
```
Result: "1 spam"

```
%[(name)][flags][width][.precision]code
```
General target format

*flags* include "−" (left justify), "+" (numeric sign), and "0"
(zero fill); *width* is total field width; *precision* gives digits
after "."; and *code* is a character from Table 8. Also see the
sections "The string Module and Methods" and "The re Pattern-Matching Module," and related built-in functions. Hint:
%s converts any object to its print representation string.

*Table 8. % string formatting codes*

| Code | Meaning | Code | Meaning |
|------|---------|------|---------|
| s | String (or any object) | X | x with uppercase |
| r | s, but uses repr( ) not str( ) | e | Floating-point exponent |
| c | Character | E | e with uppercase |
| d | Decimal (integer) | f | Floating-point decimal |
| i | Integer | F | f with uppercase |
| u | Unsigned (integer) | g | Floating-point e or f |
| o | Octal integer | G | Floating-point E or F |
| x | Hex integer | % | Literal '%' |

## String methods

Starting in Python 2.0, most of the functions previously available in the standard string module are now also available as methods of string objects. If X references a string object, then a string module function call:

```
import string
res = string.replace(X, 'span', 'spam')
```

is usually equivalent to a string method call:

```
res = X.replace('span', 'spam')
```

But string methods require no module imports. Note that the string.join(list, delim) operation becomes a method of the delimiter string: delim.join(list).

Table 9 lists available string method calls. String methods that modify text always return a new string and never modify the object in-place (strings are immutable). See the later section "The string Module and Methods" for additional details on most of the calls in this table.

Note that some string module calls many not be available as string methods, and some string methods are not available in the string module. The following calls in Table 9 are currently unique: endswith and startswith (suffix and prefix match); splitlines (split on line breaks); title (similar to string.capwords); encode (string encoding—see "Unicode strings"); and all is*() Boolean content tests. The is*() Boolean tests work on strings of any length.

*Table 9. String method calls*

```
S.capitalize()
S.center(width)
S.count(sub [, start [, end]])
S.encode([encoding [,errors]])
S.endswith(suffix [, start [, end]])
S.expandtabs([tabsize])
S.find(sub [, start [, end]])
S.index(sub [, start [, end]])
S.isalnum()
S.isalpha()
S.isdigit()
S.islower()
S.isspace()
S.istitle()
S.isupper()
S.join(seq)
S.ljust(width)
S.lower()
S.lstrip()
S.replace(old, new [, maxsplit])
S.rfind(sub [,start [,end]])
S.rindex(sub [, start [, end]])
S.rjust(width)
S.rstrip()
S.split([sep [,maxsplit]])
S.splitlines([keepends])
S.startswith(prefix [, start [, end]])
S.strip()
S.swapcase()
```

*Table 9. String method calls (continued)*

```
S.title()
S.translate(table [, deletechars])
S.upper()
```

## Unicode strings

Python supports Unicode (wide) character strings, which represent each character with 16 bits, not 8.

**Constants.** Unicode strings are written as u"*string*". Arbitrary Unicode characters may be written using a new (in 2.0) escape sequence, \u*HHHH*, where *HHHH* is a four-digit hexadecimal number from 0000 to FFFF. The traditional \x*HH* escape sequence can also be used, and octal escapes can be used for characters up to +01FF, which is represented by \777.

**Operations.** Like normal strings, all immutable sequence operations apply. Normal and Unicode string objects may be freely mixed; combining 8-bit and Unicode strings always coerces to Unicode, using the default ASCII encoding (e.g., the result of 'a' + u'bc' is u'abc'). Mixed-type operations assume the 8-bit string contains a 7-bit U.S. ASCII data. The encode string method applies a desired encoding scheme to Unicode strings. A handful of related modules (e.g., codecs) and built-in functions are also available. See the Python Library Reference for details.

# Lists

Lists are mutable (changeable) arrays of object references, accessed by offset.

## Constants

Lists are written as comma-separated series of values enclosed in square brackets.

[] An empty list

[0, 1, 2, 3]
> A four-item list: indexes 0..3

alist = ['spam', [42, 3.1415], 1.23, {}]
> Nested sublists: alist[1][0] fetches 42

## Operations

All sequence operations (see Table 3), plus all mutable sequence operations (see Table 4), plus the following list methods:

alist.append(x)
> Inserts the single object x at the end of alist, changing the list in-place.

alist.sort([func])
> Sorts alist in-place in ascending order, or per a passed-in two-argument comparison function func (which returns −1, 0, or +1, to mean before, same, or after ordering). Note: sort + reverse is quicker than sort(func).

alist.reverse( )
> Reverses items in alist in-place.

alist.index(x)
> Returns the offset of the first occurrence of object x in alist; raises an exception if not found. A search method.

alist.insert(i, x)
> Inserts object x into alist at offset i (like alist[i:i] = [x], for positive i).

alist.count(x)
> Returns the number of occurrences of x in alist.

alist.remove(x)
> Deletes the first occurrence of object x from alist; raises an exception if not found.

---

```
alist.extend(x)
```
Inserts each item in any sequence x at the end of alist in-place (an in-place "+"). Like `alist[len(alist):] = list(x)`.

```
alist.pop([i])
```
Deletes and returns the last (or offset i) item in alist. Use with append to implement stacks. Same as `x=alist[i]; del alist[i]; return x`, where i defaults to −1, the last item.

## List comprehension expressions

A list literal enclosed in square brackets ([...]) may be a simple list of expressions or a list comprehension expression of the following form:

```
[ expression for expr1 in sequence1 [if condition]
             for expr2 in sequence2 [if condition] ...
                 for exprN in sequenceN [if condition] ]
```

List comprehensions construct result lists: they collect all values of *expression*, for each iteration of all nested for loops, for which each optional *condition* is true. The second through *n*th for loops and all if parts are optional, and *expression* and *condition* may use variables assigned by nested for loops. Names bound inside the comprehension are created in the scope where the comprehension resides.

Comprehensions are similar to the map built-in function:

```
>>> [ord(x) for x in 'spam']
[115, 112, 97, 109]
>>> map(ord, 'spam')
[115, 112, 97, 109]
```

but can often avoid creating a temporary function:

```
>>> [x**2 for x in range(5)]
[0, 1, 4, 9, 16]
>>> map((lambda x: x**2), range(5))
[0, 1, 4, 9, 16]
```

Comprehensions with conditions are similar to `filter`:

```
>>> [x for x in range(5) if x % 2 == 0]
[0, 2, 4]
>>> filter((lambda x: x % 2 == 0), range(5))
[0, 2, 4]
```

Comprehensions with nested `for` loops are like normal `for`:

```
>>> [y for x in range(3) for y in range(3)]
[0, 1, 2, 0, 1, 2, 0, 1, 2]

>>> res = []
>>> for x in range(3):
...     for y in range(3):
...         res.append(y)
>>> res
[0, 1, 2, 0, 1, 2, 0, 1, 2]
```

# Dictionaries

Dictionaries are mutable tables of object references, accessed by key, not position. They are unordered collections, implemented internally as dynamically expandable hash tables.

## Constants

Dictionaries are written as comma-separated series of *key*: *value* pairs inside curly braces. Assigning to new keys generates new entries. Any immutable object can be a key (e.g., string, number, tuple); class instances can be keys if they inherit hashing protocol methods; tuple keys support compound values (e.g., `D[(1,2,3)]`).

`{}` An empty dictionary

`{'spam': 2, 'eggs': 3}`
    A two-item dictionary: keys `'spam'` and `'eggs'`

`adict = { 'info': { 42: 1, type("): 2 }, 'spam': [] }`
    Nested dictionaries: `adict['info'][42]` fetches 1

## Operations

All mapping operations (see Table 5), plus the following dictionary-specific methods:

adict.has_key(k)
> Returns 1 (true) if adict has a key k, or 0 otherwise.

adict.keys( )
> A new list holding all of adict's keys.[*]

adict.values( )
> A new list holding all the stored values in adict.

adict.items( )
> A new list of tuple pairs (key, value), one for each entry in adict.

adict.clear( )
> Removes all items from adict.

adict.copy( )
> Returns a shallow (top-level) copy of adict.

dict1.update(dict2)
> Merges all of dict2's entries into dict1, in-place. Like for (k, v) in dict2.items( ): dict1[k] = v.

adict.get(key [, default])
> Similar to adict[key], but returns default (or None if no default) instead of raising an exception when key is not found in adict.

adict.setdefault(key, [, default])
> Same as adict.get(key, default), but also assigns key key to default if it is not found in adict.

adict.popitem( )
> Remove and return an arbitrary (key, value) pair.

---

[*] In Python 2.2, dictionary keys can also be iterated over directly. for key in dict: now has an effect similar to for key in dict.keys( ):.

# Tuples

Tuples are immutable arrays of object references, accessed by offset.

## Constants

Tuples are written as comma-separated series of values enclosed in parentheses. The enclosing parentheses may sometimes be omitted (e.g., in for loop headers and = assignments).

`( )`  An empty tuple

`(0,)`
> A one-item tuple (not a simple expression)

`(0, 1, 2, 3)`
> A four-item tuple

`0, 1, 2, 3`
> Another four-item tuple (same as prior line); not valid in function calls

`atuple = ('spam', (42, 'eggs'))`
> Nested tuples: `atuple[1][1]` fetches `'eggs'`

## Operations

All sequence operations (see Table 3).

# Files

The built-in open function creates a stdio file object, the most common file interface. File objects export the method calls in the next section. Also see the open function in "Built-in Functions," the anydbm, shelve, and pickle modules in "Object Persistence Modules," the os module descriptor-based file functions and the os.path directory path tools in "The os System Module," and the Python SQL database API in "Python Portable SQL Database API."

---

## Input files

```
input = open('data.txt', 'r')
```

Creates input file ('r' means read). The filename string (e.g., 'data.txt') maps to the current working directory, unless it includes a directory path prefix (e.g., 'c:\\dir\\ data.txt'). The mode argument (e.g., 'r') is optional and defaults to 'r'.

```
input.read()
```

Reads entire file, returning its contents as a single string. In text mode ('r'), line-ends are translated to '\n'. In binary mode ('rb'), the result string may contain non-printable characters (e.g., '\0').

```
input.read(N)
```

Reads at most N bytes (1 or more).

```
input.readline()
```

Reads next line (through end-of-line marker).

```
input.readlines()
```

Reads entire file into a list of line strings.*

```
input.xreadlines()
```

Optimized readlines. Loads only a few lines at a time into memory, when used in a for loop header.

## Output files

```
output = open('/tmp/spam', 'w')
```

Creates output file ('w' means write).

```
output.write(S)
```

Writes string S onto file (all bytes in S). In text mode, '\n' is translated to the platform-specific line-end marker sequence. In binary mode, the string may contain non-

---

* In Python 2.2, files can also be iterated over directly. for line in fileobj: now has an effect similar to for line in fileobj.readlines():, but the file iterator may be more efficient.

printable bytes (e.g., use `'a\0b\0c'` to write a string of five bytes, two of which are binary zero).

`output.writelines(L)`
   Writes all strings in list L onto file.

## Any files

`file.close()`
   Manual close to free resources (Python currently auto-closes files when they are garbage collected).

`file.tell()`
   Returns the file's current position (like C's ftell).

`file.seek(offset [, whence])`
   Sets the current file position to offset for random access (like C's fseek). whence may be 0 (offset from front), 1 (offset +/– from current position), or 2 (offset from end). whence defaults to 0.

`file.isatty()`
   Returns 1 if the file is connected to a tty-like interactive device.

`file.flush()`
   Flushes the file's stdio buffer (like C's fflush). Useful for buffered pipes, if another process (or human) is reading. Also useful for files created and read in the same process.

`file.truncate([size])`
   Truncates file to at most size bytes (or current position if no size is passed). Not available on all platforms.

`file.fileno()`
   Gets file number (descriptor integer) for file. This roughly converts file objects to descriptors that may be passed to tools in the os module. Hints: use os.fdopen to convert a descriptor to a file object, socketobj.makefile to convert a socket to a file object, and StringIO.StringIO to convert a string to an object with a file-like interface.

## Attributes

`file.closed`
> True if file has been closed

`file.mode`
> Mode string (e.g., `'r'`) passed to open function

`file.name`
> String name of corresponding external file

## Notes

- Some file open modes (e.g., `'r+'`) allow a file to be both input and output, and others (e.g., `'rb'`) specify binary-mode transfer to suppress line-end marker conversions. See open in "Built-in Functions."

- File transfer operations occur at the current file position, but seek method calls reposition the file for random access.

- File transfers may be made *unbuffered*: see open in "Built-in Functions" and the -u command-line flag in "Command-Line Options."

# Type Conversions

Tables 10 and 11 define built-in tools for converting from one type to another.

*Table 10. Sequence converters*

| Converter | Converts from | Converts to |
|---|---|---|
| `list(X)`<br>`map(None, X)`<br>`[n for n in X]` | String, tuple, user-defined sequence | List |
| `tuple(X)` | String, list, user-defined sequence | Tuple |
| `''.join(X)`<br>`string.join(X, '')` | List or tuple of strings | String |

*Table 11. String/object converters*

| Converter | Converts from | Converts to |
|---|---|---|
| eval(S) | String | Any object with a syntax (expression) |
| string.atoi(S)<br>string.atof(S)<br>string.atol(S) | String | Integer, float, long |
| int(S)[a]<br>float(S)<br>long(S) | String or number | Integer, float, long |
| repr(X)<br>str(X)<br>`X` (backquotes) | Any Python object | String |
| X % Y (string formatting) | Objects with format codes | String |

[a] In Release 2.2, converter functions (e.g., int, float, str) are also available as class constructors. See 2.2 release notes for more details.

# Statements and Syntax

This section describes the rules for syntax and variable names.

## Syntax Rules

Here are the basic rules for writing Python programs:

*Control flow*
> Statements execute one after another, unless control-flow statements are used (if, while, for, raise, calls, etc.).

*Blocks*
> A block is delimited by indenting all of its statements the same amount, with spaces or tabs. A tab counts for enough spaces to move the column to a multiple of 8. Blocks can appear on the same line as a statement header if they are simple statements.

*Statements*
> A statement ends at the end of a line, but may continue over multiple lines if a physical line ends with a \, an

unclosed ( ), [ ], or { } pair, or an unclosed, triple-quoted string. Multiple simple statements can appear on a line if separated with a semicolon (;).

*Comments*
Comments start with a # (not in a string constant) and span to the end of the line.

*Documentation strings*
If a function, module file, or class begins with a string constant, it is stored in the object's __doc__ attribute. See the pydoc module and script in the Python Library Reference for automated extraction and display tools.

*Whitespace*
Generally significant only to the left of code, where indentation is used to group blocks. Blank lines and space are otherwise ignored except as token separators and within string constants.

# Name Rules

This section contains the rules for user-defined names (i.e., variables) in programs.

## Name format

*Structure*
User-defined names start with a letter or underscore (_), followed by any number of letters, digits, or underscores.

*Reserved words*
User-defined names cannot be the same as any Python reserved word listed in Table 12.[*]

*Case sensitivity*
User-defined names and reserved words are always case-sensitive: "SPAM", "spam", and "Spam" are all different names.

---

[*] In the Jython Java-based implementation, user-defined names can sometimes be the same as reserved words.

*Unused tokens*

Python does not use the characters @, $, or ? in its syntax, though they may appear in string constants and comments.

*Creation*

User-defined names are created by assignment but must exist when referenced. See the section "Namespace and Scope Rules" later in the book.

*Table 12. Reserved words*

| and | assert | break | class | continue |
|-----|--------|-------|-------|----------|
| def | del | elif | else | except |
| exec | finally | for | from | global |
| if | import | in | is | lambda |
| not | or | pass | print | raise |
| return | try | while | yield[a] | |

[a] `yield` was added as a future item in 2.2 (enabled with `from __future__ import generators`); it is reserved in 2.2 only if enabled and will be made a true reserved word in 2.3.

## Name conventions

- Names that begin and end with two underscores (for example, `__init__`) have a special meaning to the interpreter but are not reserved words.

- Names beginning with one underscore (e.g., `_X`) and assigned at the top level of a module are not copied out by `from...*` imports (see also the `__all__` module export names list, mentioned in "The from Statement" and "Pseudo-Private Attributes").

- Names beginning but not ending with two underscores (e.g., `__X`) within a `class` statement are prefixed with the enclosing class's name (see "Pseudo-Private Attributes").

- The name that is just a single underscore (`_`) is used in the interactive interpreter (only) to store the result of the last evaluation.

- Built-in function and exception names (e.g., open, SyntaxError) are not reserved words, live in the last-searched scope, and may be reassigned to hide the built-in meaning in the current scope (e.g., open=42).
- Class names commonly begin with an uppercase letter (e.g., MyClass).
- The first (leftmost) argument in a class method function is commonly named self.

# Specific Statements

The following sections describe all Python statements. Each section lists the statement's syntax formats, followed by usage details. For compound statements, each appearance of a *suite* in a statement format stands for one or more other statements, possibly indented as a block under a header line. A suite must be indented under a header if it contains another compound statement (if, while, etc.); otherwise, it can appear on the same line as the statement header. The following are both valid constructs:

```
if x < 42:
    print x
    while x: x = x -1

if x < 42: print x
```

## Assignment

```
target = expression
target1 = target2 = expression
target1, target2 = expression1, expression2
target1, target2,...  = same-length-sequence
(target1, target2,...) = same-length-sequence
[target1, target2,...] = same-length-sequence
```

Stores references to objects in targets. Expressions yield objects. Targets may be simple names (X), qualified attributes (X.attr), or indexes and slices (X[i], X[i:j]).

The second format assigns *expression* object to each target. The third format pairs targets with expressions, left to right. The last three formats assign components of any sequence to corresponding targets, from left to right. The sequence on the right must be the same length, but can be any type.

## Augmented assignment

As of Python 2.0, a set of additional assignment statement formats, listed in Table 13, are available. Known as "augmented assignment," these formats imply a binary expression plus an assignment. For instance, the following two formats are roughly equivalent:

```
X = X + Y
X += Y
```

but the reference to target X needs to be evaluated only once, and in-place operations may be applied for mutables as an optimization (e.g., list1 += list2 automatically calls list1.extend(list2), instead of the slower concatenation operation implied by +). Classes may overload in-place assignments with method names that begin with an "i" (e.g., __iadd__ for +=, __add__ for +). The format X //= Y (floor division) is new in 2.2.

*Table 13. Augmented assignment statements*

| | | | |
|---|---|---|---|
| X += Y | X &= Y | X -= Y | X \|= Y |
| X *= Y | X ^= Y | X /= Y | X »= Y |
| X %= Y | X «= Y | X **= Y | X //= Y |

## Expressions

```
expression
function([value, name=value, ...])
object.method([value, name=value, ...])
```

Any expression can appear as a statement (but statements cannot appear as expressions). Expressions are commonly used for running functions and for interactive-mode printing.

In function and method calls, actual arguments are separated by commas and are normally matched to arguments in function def headers by position. Calls may optionally list specific argument names in functions to receive passed values, by using the *name=value* keyword syntax.

### apply( )-like call syntax

As of Python 2.0, special syntax can be used in function and method call argument lists to achieve the same effect as an apply( ) built-in function call. If *args* and *kw* are a tuple and a dictionary, respectively, the following are equivalent:

```
apply(f, args, kw)
f(*args, **kw)
```

Both formats call function f with positional arguments *args* and keyword arguments *kw*. The latter format is intended to be symmetric with function header arbitrary-argument syntax such as def f(*args, **kw):.

## The print Statement

```
print [value [, value]* [,]]
print >> fileobj [, value [, value]* [,]]
```

Displays the printable representation of values on stdout stream (the current setting of sys.stdout). Adds spaces between values. Trailing comma suppresses linefeed normally added at end of list. Because print simply calls the write method of the object currently referenced by sys.stdout, the following is equivalent to print X:

```
import sys
sys.stdout.write(str(X) + '\n')
```

To redirect print text to files or class objects, reassign sys.stdout to any object with a write method:

```
sys.stdout = open('log', 'a')   # any object with a write( )
print "Warning-bad spam!"  # goes to the object's write( )
```

### Extended print form

As of Python 2.0, the print statement may also name an open output file-like object to be the target of the printed text (instead of sys.stdout):

```
fileobj = open('log', 'a')
print >> fileobj, "Warning-bad spam!"
```

If the file object is None, sys.stdout is used. Because sys.stdout can be reassigned, the >> form is not strictly needed; however, it can often avoid both explicit write method calls and saving and restoring the original sys.stdout value around a redirected print.

## The if Statement

```
if test:
    suite
[elif test:
    suite]*
[else:
    suite]
```

Selects from among one or more actions (statement blocks). Runs suite associated with first if or elif test that is true, or else suite if all are false.

## The while Statement

```
while test:
    suite
[else:
    suite]
```

General loops. Keeps running first suite while test at top is true. Runs else suite if loop exits without hitting a break statement.

## The for Statement

```
for target in sequence:
    suite
[else:
    suite]
```

Sequence iteration. Assigns items in *sequence* to *target* and runs first suite for each. Runs else suite if loop exits without hitting a break statement. *target* may be anything that can appear on the left side of an "=" assignment statement (e.g., for (x, y) in tuplelist:).

In 2.2, works by first trying to obtain an *iterator* object with iter(sequence) and then calling that object's next( ) method repeatedly until StopIteration is raised (see "The yield Statement"). In earlier versions, or if no iterator object can be obtained (e.g., no __iter__ method is defined), works instead by repeatedly indexing *sequence* at successively higher offsets until an IndexError is raised.

## The pass Statement

```
pass
```

Do-nothing placeholder statement, when syntactically necessary.

## The break Statement

```
break
```

Immediately exits closest enclosing while or for loop statement, skipping its associated else (if any).

## The continue Statement

```
continue
```

Immediately goes to the top of the closest enclosing while or for loop statement; resume in the loop header line.

## The del Statement

```
del name
del name[i]
del name[i:j]
del name.attribute
```

Deletes names, items, slices, and attributes. Removes bindings.

## The exec Statement

```
exec codestring [in globaldict [, localdict]]
```

Compiles and runs code strings. *codestring* is any Python statement as a string; run in namespace containing the exec, or the global/local namespace dictionaries if specified (*localdict* defaults to *globaldict*). *codestring* can also be a compiled code object. Also see compile, eval, and execfile in the section "Built-in Functions."

## The def Statement

```
def name([arg, arg=value,... *arg, **arg]):
    suite
```

Makes new functions. Creates a function object and assigns it to variable *name*. Each call to a function object generates a new, local scope, where assigned names are local to the function call by default (unless declared global). See also the section "Namespace and Scope Rules" later in the book. Arguments are passed by assignment; in a def header, they may be defined by any of the formats in Table 14.

*Table 14. Argument definition formats*

| Argument format | Interpretation |
| --- | --- |
| arg | Simple name, matched by name or position |
| arg=value | Default value if arg not passed |
| *arg | Collects extra positional args |
| **arg | Collects extra keyword args passed by name |

Mutable default argument values are evaluated once at def statement time, not on each call, so may retain state between calls (but classes are better state-retention tools):

```
>>> def grow(a, b=[]):
...     b.append(a)
...     print b
...
>>> grow(1); grow(2)
[1]
[1, 2]
```

### lambda expressions

Functions may also be created with the lambda expression form: lambda *arg, arg,...: expression*. In lambda, *arg* is as in def, *expression* is the implied return value, and the generated function is simply returned as the lambda result to be called later, instead of being assigned to a variable. Because lambda is an expression, not a statement, it may be used in places that a def cannot be (e.g., within an argument list of a call).

## The return Statement

```
return [expression]
```

Exits the enclosing function and returns *expression* value as the result of the call to the function. Hint: return a tuple for multiple-value function results.

## The yield Statement

```
yield expression
```

Optional in 2.2; enable with from __future__ import generators. Suspend function state and return *expression*. On the next iteration, the function's prior state is restored, and control resumes immediately after the yield statement. Use a return statement with no value to end the iteration, or simply fall off the end of the function.

```
def generate_ints(N):
    for i in xrange(N):
        yield i
```

### Generators and iterators

In 2.2, functions containing a yield statement are compiled as *generators*; when called, they return a generator object that supports the iterator interface (i.e., a next( ) method).

*Iterators* are objects returned by the iter(X) built-in function; they define a next( ) method, which returns the next item in the iteration or raises a StopIteration exception to end the iteration. Classes may provide an __iter__ method to overload the iter(X) built-in function call; if defined, the result is used to step through objects in for loops, rather than the traditional __getitem__ indexing overload scheme.

## The global Statement

```
global name [, name]*
```

Namespace declaration: inside a class or function, treats appearances of *name* as references to a global (module-level) variable by that name—whether it is assigned or not. Because of Python scope rules, you need to declare only global names that are assigned within a def (global references are automatically found in the enclosing module).

## The import Statement

```
import module [, module]*
import [package.]* module [, [package.]* module]*
import module as name
```

Module access: imports a module as a whole. Modules contain names fetched by qualification (e.g., *module.attribute*). module names the target module—a Python file or compiled module located in a directory in sys.path (PYTHONPATH), without its filename suffix (e.g., omit the ".py"). Assignments at the top level of a Python file create module object attributes. The as clause assigns a variable *name* to the imported module object; useful to provide shorter synonyms for long module names.

Import operations compile a file's source to byte-code if needed (and save it in a *.pyc* file if possible), then execute the compiled code from top to bottom to generate module object attributes by assignment. Use the reload built-in function to force recompilation and execution of already-loaded modules; see also __import__ used by import, in the later section "Built-in Functions."

In the Jython implementation, imports may also name Java class libraries; Jython generates a Python module wrapper that interfaces with the Java library. In Standard (C) Python, imports may also load compiled C and C++ extensions.

### Package imports

If used, *package* prefix names give enclosing *directory* names, and module dotted paths reflect directory hierarchies. An import of the form import dir1.dir2.mod loads the file at directory path dir1/dir2/mod.py, where dir1 must be contained by a directory listed on PYTHONPATH. Each directory through which an import descends must have a (possibly empty) __init__.py file that serves as the directory level's module namespace. All names assigned in __init__.py files become attributes of the directory's module object. Directory packages can resolve conflicts caused by the linear nature of PYTHONPATH.

## The from Statement

```
from [package.]* module import name [, name]*
from [package.]* module import *
from module import name as othername
```

Module names access: import (copy) variable names out of a module and use them later without enclosing module name qualification. The from mod import * format copies *all* names assigned at the top level of the module, except names with a single leading underscore or names not listed in the module's __all__ list-of-strings attribute (if defined).

If used, the as clause creates a name synonym. If used, *package* import paths work the same as in import statements (e.g., from dir1.dir2.mod import X), but the package path needs to be listed only in the from itself. Due to new scoping rules, the "*" format generates warnings in 2.2 if it appears nested in a function or class.

The from statement is also used to enable future (but still experimental) language additions, with from __future__ import *featurename*. This format must appear only at the top of a module file (preceded only by an optional doc string).

## The class Statement

```
class name [( super [, super]* )]:
    suite
```

Makes new class objects, which are factories for instance objects. Builds a new class object and assigns it to variable *name*. The class statement introduces a new local name scope, and all names assigned in the class statement generate class object attributes shared by all instances of the class. Important class features include the following (see also the later sections "Object-Oriented Programming" and "Operator Overloading Methods"):

- Superclasses from which the new class inherits attributes are listed in parentheses in the header (e.g., class Sub(Super1, Super2):).

- Assignments in the suite generate class attributes inherited by instances: nested def statements make methods, assignment statements make simple class members, etc.

- Calling the class generates instance objects. Each instance object has its own attributes and inherits the attributes of the class and all of its superclasses.
- Specially named method definitions overload operations.

## The try Statement

```
try:
    suite
[except [name [, data]]:
    suite]*
[else:
    suite]

try:
    suite
finally:
    suite
```

Catches exceptions. try statements may specify except clauses with suites that serve as handlers for exceptions raised during the try suite, else clauses that run if no exception occurs during the try suite, and finally clauses that run whether an exception happens or not.

Exceptions may be raised by Python, or explicitly (see also the raise statement). In except clauses, an extra variable name (*data*) can be used to intercept an extra data item raised with the exception name. Table 15 lists all the clauses that may appear in a try statement. finally cannot be mixed with except or else.

*Table 15. try statement clause formats*

| Clause format | Interpretation |
| --- | --- |
| except: | Catch all (other) exceptions |
| except *name*: | Catch a specific exception only |
| except *name, value*: | Catch exception and extra data |
| except (*name1, name2*): | Catch any of the exceptions |
| else: | Run if no exceptions raised |
| finally: | Always run on the way out |

Common variations include:

except *classname*, X:
: Catch a class exception, and assign X to the raised instance.

except (*name1, name2, name2*), X:
: Catch any of the exceptions, and assign *X* to the extra data.

## The raise Statement

raise *string*
: Matches except that names same string object.

raise *string, data*
: Passes extra *data* object with exception (default is None); assigned to variable X in an except string, X: try statement clause.

raise *instance*
: Same as raise instance.__class__, instance.

raise *class, instance*
: Matches except that names this *class*, or any of its super-classes. Passes the class instance object as extra data with exception, to be assigned to *X* in an except *class*, *X*: try statement clause.

raise
: Re-raises the current exception.

Triggers exceptions. Control jumps to the matching except clause of the most recently entered matching try statement, or to the top level of process (where it ends the program and prints a standard error message). May use to raise built-in or user-defined exceptions. Without arguments, re-raises the most recent exception. See also "Built-in Exceptions" for exceptions raised by Python.

### Class exceptions

Exceptions may be string objects (first two formats) or class instances (second two formats). try statement except clauses that name string objects are matched by string identity (is), not by value (==). try statement except clauses that name classes catch an instance of that class, as well as any of its subclasses. All built-in exceptions are now class objects.

Class exceptions support exception *categories*, which may be easily extended. Because try statements catch all subclasses when they name a superclass, exception categories may be modified by altering the set of subclasses without breaking existing try statements. The raised instance object also provides storage for extra information about the exception:

```
class General:
    def __init__(self, x):
        self.data = x
class Specific1(General): pass
class Specific2(General): pass

try:
    raise Specific1('spam')
except General, X:
    print X.data                # prints 'spam'
```

For backward compatibility with prior Python releases that only supported string exceptions, these raise formats are also allowed:

```
raise class [, arg]
raise class, (arg, arg,...)
```

These are the same as the instance format raise *class*([*arg*...]). The first format occurs when *arg* is not an instance of *class*. Python generates and raises an instance automatically, even if the raise lists only a class name (i.e., raise *Class* is the same as raise *Class*( )). It is suggested but not required that user-defined exceptions inherit from the built-in exception class Exception (see the section "Built-in Exceptions").

## The assert Statement

assert *expression* [, *message*]

Debugging checks. If *expression* is false, raises AssertionError, passing *message* as an extra data item if specified. The -0 command-line flag removes assertion logic.

# Namespace and Scope Rules

This section discusses rules for name binding and lookup. See also the "Name format" and "Name conventions" sections earlier, in "Statements and Syntax." In all cases, names are created when first assigned but must already exist when referenced. Qualified and unqualified names are resolved differently.

## Qualified Names: Object Namespaces

Qualified names (X, in object.X) are known as attributes and live in object namespaces. Assignments in some lexical scopes* initialize object namespaces (modules, classes).

Assignment: object.X = value
> Creates or alters the attribute name X in the namespace of the object being qualified.

Reference: object.X
> Searches for the attribute name X in the object, then all accessible classes above it (for instances and classes). This is the definition of *inheritance*.

## Unqualified Names: Lexical Scopes

Unqualified names (X) involve lexical scope rules. Assignments bind such names to the local scope, unless they are declared global.

Assignment: X = value
> Makes name X local: creates or changes name X in the current local scope by default. If X is declared global, creates or changes name X in the enclosing module's scope. Local variables are stored in the call stack for quick access.

Reference: X
> Prior to Release 2.2, looks for name X in at most three scopes: the current *local* scope (function), then the current *global* scope (module), then the *built-in* scope (module __builtin__). Local and global scope contexts are defined in Table 16.

---

\* Lexical scopes refer to physically nested code structures in a program's source code.

In Release 2.2 and later, looks for name X in the current local scope (function), then in the local scopes of all lexically enclosing functions (if any, from inner to outer), then in the current global scope (module), then in the built-in scope (module __builtin__). Global declarations make the search begin in the global scope instead.

*Table 16. Unqualified name scopes*

| Code context | Global scope | Local scope |
|---|---|---|
| Module | Same as local | The module itself |
| Function, method | Enclosing module | Function call |
| Class | Enclosing module | class statement |
| Script, interactive mode | Same as local | module __main__ |
| exec, eval | Caller's global (or passed in) | Caller's local (or passed in) |

## Statically nested scopes

The enclosing scope search of the last rule in the previous section is called statically nested scopes, made optional in 2.1 (use from __future__ import nested_scopes to enable), and standard in 2.2. For example, the following function works as-is in 2.2 and later, because the reference to x within f2 has access to the scope of f1:

```
def f1( ):
    x = 42
    def f2( ):
        print x
    f2( )
```

In Python versions prior to 2.2 this function fails, because name x is not local (in f2's scope), global (in the module enclosing f1), or built-in. To make such cases work prior to 2.2, default arguments are typically used to retain values from the immediately enclosing scope (defaults are evaluated before entering a def):

```
def f1( ):
    x = 42
```

```
    def f2(x=x):
        print x
    f2()
```

This rule also applies to lambda expressions, which imply a nested scope just like def and are more commonly nested in practice:

```
def func():
    x = 42
    action = (lambda n: x ** n)          # works in 2.2

def func():
    x = 42
    action = (lambda n, x=x: x ** n)   # use before 2.2
```

Scopes nest arbitrarily, but only enclosing functions (not classes) are searched.

```
def f1():
    x = 42
    def f2():
        def f3():
            print x      # found in f1's scope
        f3()
    f2()
```

As a consequence of this change in 2.2, the following constructs may no longer be valid within a function body: from module import *, and exec statements without explicit namespace dictionaries. Both constructs can assign unknown names and so prevent the compiler from detecting names defined in enclosing scopes. Programs may also fail in 2.2 if they use the same name in both the global and a lexically enclosing function's scope; the enclosing function's name now hides the global.

# Object-Oriented Programming

Classes are Python's main OOP tool. They support multiple instances, attribute inheritance, and operator overloading.

# Classes and Instances

### Class objects provide default behavior

- The class statement creates a *class* object and assigns it to a name.

- Assignments inside class statements create class *attributes*, which export object state and behavior.

- Class *methods* are nested defs, with special first arguments to receive the instance.

### Instance objects are generated from classes

- Calling a class object like a function makes a new *instance* object.

- Each instance object inherits class attributes and gets its own attribute *namespace*.

- Assignments to attributes of the first argument (e.g, self.X = V) in methods create per-instance *attributes*.

### Inheritance rules

- Inheritance happens at attribute qualification time: on object.attribute, if object is a class or instance.

- Classes inherit attributes from all classes listed in their class statement header line (superclasses). Listing more than one means *multiple inheritance*.

- Instances inherit attributes from the class from which they are generated, plus all that class's superclasses.

- Inheritance searches the instance, then its class, then all accessible superclasses (depth-first, and left-to-right), and uses the first version of an attribute name found.[*]

---

[*] In 2.2, inheritance search order may be slightly different if a superclass inherits from object (e.g., class A(object)) but is still strictly depth-first and then left-to-right otherwise; see 2.2 release notes.

## Pseudo-Private Attributes

By default, all attribute names in modules and classes are visible everywhere. Special conventions allow some limited data hiding, but are mostly designed to prevent name collisions. See also "Name conventions" in "Statements and Syntax."

### Module privates

Names in modules with a single underscore (e.g., _X), and those not listed on the module's __all__ list, are not copied over when a client uses from module import *. This is not strict privacy, though, as such names can still be accessed apart from the from..* statement.

### Class privates

In Python 1.5 and later, names anywhere within class statements with two leading underscores only (e.g., __X) are mangled at compile time to include the enclosing class name as a prefix (e.g., _Class__X). The added class-name prefix localizes such names to the enclosing class and thus makes them distinct in both the self instance object and the class hierarchy.

This especially helps to avoid clashes that arise in the single instance object at the bottom of the inheritance chain (all assignments to self.attr anywhere in a framework change the single instance namespace). This is not strict privacy, though, as such attributes can still be accessed via the mangled name.

# Operator Overloading Methods

Classes intercept and implement built-in operations by providing specially named method functions, which all start and end with two underscores. These names are not reserved and may be inherited from superclasses as usual. At most one is located and called per operation.

Python automatically calls a class's overloading methods when instances appear in expressions and other contexts. For example, if a class defines a method named \_\_getitem\_\_, and X is an instance of this class, then the expression X[i] is equivalent to the method call X.\_\_getitem\_\_(i).

Overloading method names are sometimes arbitrary: a class's \_\_add\_\_ method need not perform an addition (or concatenation). Moreover, classes generally may mix numeric and collection methods and mutable and nonmutable operations.

## For All Types

\_\_init\_\_(self [, arg]*)
> On class(args...). Constructor: initializes the new instance, self.

\_\_del\_\_(self)
> On instance garbage collection. Cleans up when instance is freed. Embedded objects are automatically freed when parent is (unless referenced from elsewhere).

\_\_repr\_\_(self)
> On `self`, repr(self), print self (if no \_\_str\_\_).*
> Returns string representation.

\_\_str\_\_(self)
> On str(self), print self (or uses \_\_repr\_\_ if defined).
> Returns string representation.

\_\_cmp\_\_(self, other), \_\_rcmp\_\_
> On self > x, x == self, cmp(self, x), etc. Called for all comparisons for which no more specific method (such as \_\_lt\_\_) is defined or inherited (see rich comparison methods below). Returns −1, 0, or 1 for self less than, equal to, or greater than other. If no rich comparison or \_\_cmp\_\_ methods are defined, class instances compare by

---

* If no \_\_str\_\_ is defined, the object prints as the result of \_\_repr\_\_ (or a default representation, if no \_\_repr\_\_). By convention, \_\_str\_\_ is a user-friendly format and \_\_repr\_\_ is an "official" and parseable format.

their identity (address in memory). Note: `__rcmp__` right-side method is no longer supported as of Release 2.1.

`__hash__(self)`
> On `dictionary[self]`, `hash(self)`. Returns a unique and unchanging integer hash-key.

`__call__(self [, arg]*)`
> On `self(args...)`, when instance is called like a function.

`__getattr__(self, name)`
> On `self.name`, when name is an undefined attribute access (not called if name exists in or is inherited by `self`). name is a string. Returns object or raises `AttributeError`.

`__setattr__(self, name, value)`
> On `self.name=value` (all attribute assignments). Hint: assign through `__dict__` key to avoid loops: `self.attr=x` statement within a `__setattr__` calls `__setattr__` again, but `self.__dict__['attr']=x` does not.

`__delattr__(self, name)`
> On `del self.name` (all attribute deletions).

`__lt__(self, other)`
`__le__(self, other)`
`__eq__(self, other)`
`__ne__(self, other)`
`__gt__(self, other)`
`__ge__(self, other)`
> Respectively, on `self < other`, `self <= other`, `self == other`, `self != other` and `self <> other`, `self > other`, `self >= other`. Added in 2.1, these are knows as *rich comparison* methods and are called for comparison operators in preference to `__cmp__` (see earlier). For example, `X < Y` calls `X.__lt__(Y)` if defined; else, tries `X.__cmp__(Y)`.

These methods can return any value, but if the comparison operator is used in a Boolean context, the return value is interpreted as a Boolean result for the operator. These methods may also return the special object

`NotImplemented`, which forces Python to revert to the general `__cmp__` method.

There are no right-side (swapped-argument) versions of these methods to be used when the left argument does not support the operation but the right argument does. `__lt__` and `__gt__` are each other's reflection, `__le__` and `__ge__` are each other's reflection, and `__eq__` and `__ne__` are their own reflections.

## For Collections (Sequences, Mappings)

`__len__(self)`
> On `len(self)`, truth-value tests. Returns sequence or mapping collection size. Zero length means false. For Boolean tests, looks for `__nonzero__` first, then `__len__`, then considered true.

`__contains__(self, item)`
> On `item in self`. New in 2.0. Sequence membership test (else uses `__iter__` if defined, else uses `__getitem__`). Returns 1 or 0 for true or false.

`__iter__(self)`
> On `iter(self)`. New in 2.2. Sequence iteration generator. Returns an object with a `next( )` method (possibly `self`). The result object's `next( )` method is called repeatedly in all iteration contexts (e.g., for loops). This method should raise `StopIteration` to terminate the progression. See also "Generators and iterators" in the earlier section "The yield Statement."

As of Python 2.0, the following three methods may also be called for slice operations. For sequence types, the accepted keys should be integers and slice objects. Slice objects have the attributes `start`, `stop`, and `step`, any of which may be `None`. See also the slice methods later in this section.

`__getitem__(self, key)`
> On `self[key]`, `x in self`, `for x in self`. Implements all indexing-related operations. Membership and iteration

(in and for) repeatedly index from 0 until IndexError, unless __iter__ is defined. In 2.0, may also be passed a slice object for some slice operations.

__setitem__(self, key, value)
>   On self[key]=value. Assignment to collection key or index.

__delitem__(self, key)
>   On del self[key]. Index/key component deletion.

As of Python 2.0, the following three methods are considered deprecated, but are still supported. They are called only when a simple two-item slice with a single colon is used and the slice method is defined. For slice operations involving extended three-item slice notation, or in the absence of the slice method, __getitem__, __setitem__, or __delitem__ is called instead, with a slice object as its argument.

__getslice__(self, low, high)
>   On self[low:high]. Sequence slicing. This format is considered deprecated as of Python 2.0. If no __getslice__ is found or an extended three-item sliced is used, a *slice object* is created and passed to the __getitem__ method.

__setslice__(self, low, high, seq)
>   On self[low:high]=seq. Sequence slice assignment.

__delslice__(self, low, high)
>   On del self[low:high]. Sequence slice deletion.

## For Numbers (Binary Operators)

### Basic binary methods

__add__(self, other)
>   On self + other. Numeric addition, or sequence concatenation.

__sub__(self, other)
>   On self - other.

`__mul__(self, other)`
> On self * other. Numeric multiplication, or sequence repetition.

`__div__(self, other)`
> On self / other. Classic division (integer / truncates).

`__floordiv__(self, other)`
> On self // other. Truncating (always) division.

`__truediv__(self, other)`
> On self / other. True division (optional in 2.2, standard in 3.0).

`__mod__(self, other)`
> On self % other.

`__divmod__(self, other)`
> On divmod(self, other).

`__pow__(self, other [, modulo])`
> On pow(self, other [, modulo]), self ** other.

`__lshift__(self, other)`
> On self << other.

`__rshift__(self, other)`
> On self >> other.

`__and__(self, other)`
> On self & other.

`__xor__(self, other)`
> On self ^ other.

`__or__(self, other)`
> On self | other.

## Right-side binary methods

`__radd__(self, other)`
`__rsub__(self, other)`
`__rmul__(self, other)`
`__rdiv__(self, other)`

```
__rfloordiv__(self, other)
__rtruediv__(self, other)
__rmod__(self, other)
__rdivmod__(self, other)
__rpow__(self, other)
__rlshift__(self, other)
__rrshift__(self, other)
__rand__(self, other)
__rxor__(self, other)
__ror__(self, other)
```

Right-side operator methods. Binary operator methods each have a right-side variant that starts with an "r" prefix; e.g., __add__ and __radd__. Right-side variants have the same argument lists, but self is on the right side of the operator. For instance, self + other calls self.__add__(other), but other + self invokes self.__radd__(other).

The "r" right-side method is called only when the instance is on the right and the left operand is not an instance of a class that overloads the operation:

> instance + noninstance → __add__
> instance + instance → __add__
> noninstance + instance → __radd__

If two different class instances that overload the operation appear, the class on the left is preferred. __radd__ often converts and re-adds to trigger __add__.

## Augmented binary methods

```
__iadd__(self, other)
__isub__(self, other)
__imul__(self, other)
__idiv__(self, other)
__ifloordiv__(self, other)
__itruediv__(self, other)
__imod__(self, other)
__ipow__(self, other[, modulo])
__ilshift__(self, other)
```

```
__irshift__(self, other)
__iand__(self, other)
__ixor__(self, other)
__ior__(self, other)
```
Augmented assignment (in-place) methods. Respectively, called for assignment statement formats: +=, -=, *=, /=, //=, /=, %=, **=, <<=, >>=, &=, ^=, and |=. These methods should attempt to do the operation in-place (modifying self) and return the result (which may be self). If a method is not defined, the augmented operation falls back on the normal methods. To evaluate X += Y, where X is an instance of a class that has an __iadd__, x.__iadd__(y) is called. Otherwise, __add__ and __radd__ are considered.

## For Numbers (Other Operations)

`__neg__(self)`
  On -self.

`__pos__(self)`
  On +self.

`__abs__(self)`
  On abs(self).

`__invert__(self)`
  On ~self.

`__complex__(self)`
  On complex(self).

`__int__(self)`
  On int(self).

`__long__(self)`
  On long(self).

`__float__(self)`
  On float(self).

`__oct__(self)`
  On oct(self). Returns octal string representation.

`__hex__(self)`
    On hex(self). Returns hex string representation.

`__nonzero__(self)`
    On truth-value (else uses `__len__` if defined).

`__coerce__(self, other)`
    On mixed-mode arithmetic expression, coerce( ). Returns tuple of (self, other) converted to a common type. If `__coerce__` is defined, it is generally called before any real operator methods are tried (e.g., before `__add__`). It should return a tuple containing operands converted to a common type (or None if it can't convert). See the Python Language Reference (*http://www.python.org/doc/*) for more on coercion rules.

# Built-in Functions

All built-in names (functions, exceptions, and so on) exist in the implied outer built-in scope, which corresponds to the `__builtin__` module. Because this scope is always searched last on name lookups, these functions are always available in programs without imports. However, their names are not reserved words and may be hidden by assignments to the same name in global or local scopes.

`abs(N)`
    Returns the absolute value of a number N.

`apply(func, args [, keys])`
    Calls any callable object func (a function, method, class, etc.), passing the positional arguments in tuple args, and the keyword arguments in dictionary keys. Returns func call result.

`buffer(object [, offset [, size]])`
    Returns a new buffer object for a conforming object (see the Python Library Reference).

`callable(object)`
    Returns 1 if object is callable; else, returns 0.

`chr(Int)`

> Returns a one-character string whose ASCII code is integer `Int`.

`cmp(X, Y)`

> Returns a negative integer, zero, or a positive integer to designate (X < Y), (X == Y), or (X > Y), respectively.

`coerce(X, Y)`

> Returns a tuple containing the two numeric arguments `X` and `Y` converted to a common type.

`compile(string, filename, kind)`

> Compiles `string` into a code object. `string` is a Python string containing Python program code. `filename` is a string used in error messages (and is usually the name of the file from which the code was read, or `<string>` if typed interactively). `kind` can be `exec` if `string` contains statements; `eval` if `string` is an expression; or `single`, which prints the output of an expression statement that evaluates to something other than `None`. The resulting code object can be executed with `exec` statements or `eval` calls.

`complex(real [, imag])`

> Builds a complex number object (can also be done using `J` or `j` suffix: `real+imagJ`). `imag` defaults to 0.

`delattr(object, name)`

> Deletes the attribute named `name` (a string) from `object`. Similar to `del obj.name`, but `name` is a string, not a variable (e.g., `delattr(a,'b')` is like `del a.b`).

`dir([object])`

> If no arguments, returns the list of names in the current local scope (namespace). With any object with attributes as an argument, returns the list of attribute names associated with that `object`. In 1.5 and later, works on modules, classes, and class instances, as well as built-in objects with attributes (lists, dictionaries, etc.).

divmod(X, Y)

    Returns a tuple of (X / Y, X % Y).

eval(expr [, globals [, locals]])

    Evaluates expr, which is assumed to be either a Python string containing a Python expression or a compiled code object. expr is evaluated in the namespaces of the eval call unless the globals and/or locals namespace dictionary arguments are passed. locals defaults to globals if only globals is passed. Returns expr result. Also see the compile function earlier in this section and the section "The exec Statement" earlier in this book.

execfile(filename [, globals [, locals]])

    Like eval, but runs all the code in a file whose string name is passed in as filename (instead of an expression). Unlike imports, does not create a new module object for the file. Returns None. Namespaces for code in filename are as for eval.

filter(function, sequence)

    Constructs a list from those elements of sequence for which function returns true. function takes one parameter. If function is None, returns all true items.

float(X)

    Converts a number or a string X to a floating-point number.

getattr(object, name [, default])

    Returns the value of attribute name (a string) from object. Similar to object.name, but name is a string, not a variable (e.g., getattr(a,'b') is like a.b). If the named attribute does not exist, default is returned if provided; otherwise, AttributeError is raised.

globals( )

    Returns a dictionary containing the caller's global variables (e.g., the enclosing module's names).

`hasattr(object, name)`
> Returns true if object has an attribute called name (a string); false otherwise.

`hash(object)`
> Returns the hash value of object (if it has one).

`hex(N)`
> Converts a number N to a hexadecimal string.

`id(object)`
> Returns the unique identity integer of object (i.e., its address in memory).

`__import__(name [,globals [,locals [, fromlist] ]])`
> Imports and returns a module, given its name as a string, not a variable (e.g., mod = __import__("mymod")). Generally faster than constructing and executing an import statement string with exec. This function is called by import and from statements and may be overriden to customize import operations. The second through fourth arguments have advanced roles (see the Python Library Reference).

`input([prompt])`
> Prints prompt, if given. Then reads an input line from the stdin stream (sys.stdin), evaluates it as Python code, and returns the result. Like eval(raw_input(prompt)).

`int(X [, base])`
> Converts a number or a string X to a plain integer. base may be passed only if X is a string; if base is passed as 0, the base is determined by the string contents; else, the value passed for base is used for the base of the conversion. Conversion of floating-point numbers to integers truncates toward 0.

`intern(string)`
> Enter string in the table of "interned strings" and return the interned string. Interned strings are "immortals" and serve as a performance optimization (they may be compared by fast is identity, rather than == equality).

`isinstance(object, classOrType)`
> Returns true if `object` is an instance of `classOrType`, or an instance of any subclass thereof.*

`issubclass(class1, class2)`
> Returns true if `class1` is derived from `class2`.

`iter(object [, sentinel])`
> Returns an iterator object that may be used to step through items in `object`. Iterator objects returned have a `next()` method that returns the next item or raises `StopIteration` to end the progression. If one argument, `object` is assumed to provide its own iterator or be a sequence (normal case); if two arguments, `object` is a callable that is called until it returns `sentinel`. May overload in classes with `__iter__`; may be automatically called by Python in all iteration contexts. New in 2.2.

`len(object)`
> Returns the number of items (length) in a collection `object`. Works on sequences and mappings.

`list(sequence)`
> Converter: returns a new list containing all the items in any `sequence` object. If `sequence` is already a list, returns a copy of it.

`locals()`
> Returns a dictionary containing the local variables of the caller (with one *key*:*value* entry per local).

`long(X [, base])`
> Converts a number or a string X to a long integer. `base` may be passed only if X is a string. If 0, the base is determined by the string contents; else, it is used for the base of the conversion.

---

* The second argument may also be a type object in more recent Python releases, making this function useful as an alternative type-testing tool (`isinstance(X, Type)` versus `type(X) is Type` comparisons).

```
map(function, seq [, seq]*)
```
Applies function to every item of any sequence seq and returns a list of the collected results. Example: map(abs, (1, -2)) returns [1, 2]. If additional sequence arguments are passed, function must take that many arguments, and it is passed one item from each sequence on every call. If function is None, map collects all the items into a result list. If sequences differ in length, all are padded to length of longest, with Nones.

```
max(S [, arg]*)
```
With a single argument S, returns largest item of a non-empty sequence (e.g., string, tuple, list). With more than one argument, returns largest of the arguments.

```
min(S [, arg]*)
```
With a single argument S, returns smallest item of a non-empty sequence (e.g., string, tuple, list). With more than one argument, returns smallest of the arguments.

```
oct(N)
```
Converts a number N to an octal string.

```
open(filename [, mode, [bufsize]])
```
Returns a new file object, connected to the external file named filename (a string). The filename is mapped to the current working directory, unless the filename string includes a directory prefix. The first two arguments are the same as those for C's stdio fopen function, and the file is managed by the "stdio" system.

mode defaults to 'r' if omitted, but can be 'r' for input; 'w' for output; 'a' for append; and 'rb', 'wb', or 'ab' for binary files (to suppress line-end conversions). On most systems, most of these can also have a "+" appended to open in input/output updates mode (e.g., 'r+').

bufsize defaults to an implementation-dependent value, but can be 0 for unbuffered, 1 for line-buffered, negative for system-default, or a given specific size. Buffered data transfers may not be immediately fulfilled (use flush methods to force).

ord(C)

Returns integer ASCII value of a one-character string C (or the Unicode code point, if C is a one-character Unicode string).

pow(X, Y [, Z])

Returns X to power Y [modulo Z]. Similar to the ** expression operator.

range([start,] stop [, step])

Returns a list of successive integers between start and stop. With one argument, returns integers from zero through stop-1. With two arguments, returns integers from start through stop-1. With three arguments, returns integers from start through stop-1, adding step to each predecessor in the result. start, step default to 0, 1. range(0,20,2) is a list of even integers from 0 through 18. Often used to generate offset lists for for loops.

raw_input([prompt])

Prints prompt string if given, then reads a line from the stdin input stream (sys.stdin) and returns it as a string. Strips trailing \n at end of line and raises EOFError at the end of the stdin stream.

reduce(func, list [, init])

Applies the two-argument function func to successive items from list, so as to reduce the list to a single value. If init is given, it is prepended to list.

reload(module)

Reloads, re-parses, and re-executes an already imported module in the module's current namespace. Re-execution replaces prior values of the module's attributes in-place. module must reference an existing module object; it is not a new name or a string. Useful in interactive mode if you want to reload a module after fixing it, without restarting Python. Returns the module object.

`repr(object)`

Returns a string containing a printable, and potentially parseable, representation of any `object`. Equivalent to `` `object` `` (backquotes expression).

`round(X [, N])`

Returns the floating-point value `X` rounded to `N` digits after the decimal point. `N` defaults to zero.

`setattr(object, name, value)`

Assigns value to attribute `name` (a string) in `object`. Like `object.name = value`, but `name` is a string, not a variable name (e.g., `setattr(a,'b',c)` is like `a.b=c`).

`slice([start ,] stop [, step])`

Returns a slice object representing a range, with read-only attributes `start`, `stop`, and `step`, any of which may be `None`. Arguments are the same as for `range`.

`str(object)`

Returns a string containing the printable representation of `object`.

`tuple(sequence)`

Converter: returns a new tuple with the same elements as any `sequence` passed in. If `sequence` is already a tuple, it is returned directly (not a copy).

`type(object)`

Returns a type object representing the type of `object`. Useful for type-testing in `if` statements (e.g., `if type(X)==type([]):`). See also module `types` for preset objects to compare result to (e.g., `types.ListType`), and `isinstance` earlier in this section.

`unichr(i)`

Returns the Unicode string of one character whose Unicode code is the integer `i` (e.g., `unichr(97)` returns the string `u'a'`). This is the inverse of `ord` for Unicode strings. Argument must be in range 0..65535 inclusive, or `ValueError` is raised. New in 2.0.

unicode(string [, encoding [, errors]])
    Decodes string using the codec for encoding. Error han-
dling is done according to errors. The default behavior is
to decode UTF-8 in strict mode, meaning that encoding
errors raise ValueError. See also the codecs module in the
Python Library Reference. New in 2.0.

vars([object])
    Without arguments, returns a dictionary containing the
current local scope's names. With a module, class, or
class instance object as an argument, returns a dictionary corresponding to object's attribute namespace (i.e.,
its   dict   ). Useful for "%" string formatting.

xrange([start,] stop [, step])
    Like range, but doesn't actually store entire list all at
once (generates one integer at a time). Good to use in for
loops when there is a big range and little memory. Opti-
mizes space, but generally has no speed benefit.

zip(seq [, seq]*)
    Returns a list of tuples, where each ith tuple contains the
ith element from each of the argument sequences seq.
For example, zip('ab', 'cd') returns [('a', 'c'), ('b',
'd')]. At least one sequence is required, or a TypeError is
raised. The result list is truncated to the length of the
shortest argument sequence. When there are multiple
argument sequences of the same length, zip is similar to
map with a first argument of None. With a single sequence
argument, it returns a list of one-tuples. New in 2.0.

# Built-in Exceptions

This section describes the exceptions that Python may raise
during a program's execution. Beginning with Python 1.5, all
built-in exceptions are class objects. Prior to 1.5, they were
strings. Class exceptions are mostly indistinguishable from
strings, unless they are concatenated. Built-in exceptions are
defined in the module exceptions; this module never needs

to be imported explicitly, because the exception names are provided in the built-in scope namespace. Most built-in exceptions have an associated extra data value with details.

## Base Classes (Categories)

Exception
> Root superclass for all exceptions. User-defined exceptions may be derived from this class, but this is not currently enforced or required.

StandardError
> Superclass for all other built-in exceptions except for SystemExit; subclass of the Exception root class.

ArithmeticError
> Superclass for OverflowError, ZeroDivisionError, FloatingPointError; subclass of StandardError.

LookupError
> Superclass for IndexError, KeyError; subclass of StandardError.

EnvironmentError
> Superclass for exceptions that occur outside Python (IOError, OSError); subclass of StandardError. New in Release 1.5.2.

## Specific Exceptions Raised

AssertionError
> When an assert statement's test is false.

AttributeError
> On attribute reference or assignment failure.

EOFError
> When immediate end of file is hit by input( ) or raw_input( ).

**FloatingPointError**

On floating-point operation failure.

**IOError**

On I/O or file-related operation failure.

**ImportError**

On failure of import to find module or attribute.

**IndexError**

On out-of-range sequence offset (fetch or assign).

**KeyError**

On reference to nonexistent mapping key (fetch).

**KeyboardInterrupt**

On user entry of the interrupt key (often Ctrl-C).

**MemoryError**

On recoverable memory exhaustion.

**NameError**

On failure to find a local or global unqualified name.

**NotImplementedError**

On failure to define expected protocols. New in 1.5.2.

**OSError**

On os module error (its os.error exception). New in 1.5.2.

**OverflowError**

On excessively large arithmetic operation.

**RuntimeError**

Rarely used catch-all.

**StopIteration**

On end of progression in iterator objects. New in 2.2.

**SyntaxError**

On parser encountering a syntax error.

**SystemError**

On interpreter internal error (a bug—report it).

---

SystemExit
    On a call to sys.exit( ) (can trap and ignore).

TypeError
    On passing inappropriate type to built-in operation.

UnboundLocalError
    On reference to local name that has not been assigned. New in 2.0.

UnicodeError
    On Unicode-related encoding or decoding error. New in 2.0.

ValueError
    On argument errors not covered by TypeError or other.

WindowsError
    On Windows-specific errors. New in 2.0.

ZeroDivisionError
    On division or modulus operation with 0 on the right.

## Warning category exceptions

New in 2.1. The following exceptions are used as warning categories:

Warning
    Base class for all warning categories below, subclass of Exception.

UserWarning
    Base class for warnings generated by user code.

DeprecationWarning
    Base class for warnings about deprecated features.

SyntaxWarning
    Base class for warnings about dubious syntax.

RuntimeWarning
    Base class for warnings about dubious runtime behavior.

**Warnings framework.** Warnings are issued when future language changes may break existing code in a future Python release. You can use the warnings framework to issue warnings by calling the `warnings.warn` function:

```
warnings.warn("feature X no longer supported")
```

In addition, you can add filters to disable certain warnings. You can apply a regular expression pattern to a message or module name in order to suppress warnings with varying degrees of generality. For example, you can suppress a warning about the use of the deprecated regex module by calling:

```
import warnings
warnings.filterwarnings(action = 'ignore',
                        message='.*regex module*',
                        category=DeprecationWarning,
                        module = '__main__')
```

This adds a filter that affects only warnings of the class `DeprecationWarning` triggered in the `__main__` module, applies a regular expression to match only the message that names the regex module being deprecated, and causes such warnings to be ignored. Warnings can be printed only once, printed every time the offending code is executed, or turned into exceptions that will cause the program to stop (unless the exceptions are caught). See the `warnings` module documentation in Releases 2.1 and later for more information. See also the `-W` argument in the earlier section "Command-Line Options."

# Built-in Attributes

Some objects export special attributes that are predefined by Python.[*] The following is a partial list, because many types have unique attributes all their own; see the entries for specific types in the Python Library Reference.

---

[*] In Python 2.1, you can also attach arbitrary user-defined attributes to *function* objects, simply by assigning them values.

X.\_\_dict\_\_
> Dictionary used to store object X's writable attributes.

I.\_\_methods\_\_
> List of instance object I's methods (name strings); available on many built-in types.[*]

I.\_\_members\_\_
> List of instance object I's data attributes (name strings); available on many built-in types.

I.\_\_class\_\_
> Class object from which instance I was generated. In 2.2, this also applies to object types; most objects will have a \_\_class\_\_ attribute (e.g., [].\_\_class\_\_ == list == type([])).

C.\_\_bases\_\_
> Tuple of class C's base classes, as listed in C's class statement header.

X.\_\_name\_\_
> Object X's name as a string; for classes, the name in the statement header; for modules, the name as used in imports, or "\_\_main\_\_" for the module at the top level of a program (e.g., the main file run to launch a program).

## Built-in Modules

Built-in modules are always available but must be imported to be used in client modules. To access them, use one of these formats:

- import module, and qualify module names (module.name)
- from module import name, and use module names unqualified (name)
- from module import *, and use module names unqualified (name)

---

[*] \_\_methods\_\_ and \_\_members\_\_ may disappear in Release 2.2; use the built-in dir( ) function instead.

For instance, to use name `argv` in the `sys` module, either use `import sys` and name `sys.argv`, or use `from sys import argv` and name `argv`.

There are hundreds of built-in modules; the next sections document the more commonly used ones. Listed export names followed by parentheses are functions that must be called; others are simple attributes (i.e., variable names in modules).

# The sys Interpreter Module

The `sys` module contains interpreter-related exports. It also provides access to some environment components, such as the command line, standard streams, and so on.

argv
Command-line argument strings list: [command, arguments...]. Like C's argv array.

byteorder
Indicates the native byte-order (e.g., big for big-endian). New in 2.0.

builtin_module_names
Tuple of string names of C modules compiled into this Python interpreter.

copyright
String containing the Python interpreter copyright.

dllhandle
Python DLL integer handle; Windows only (see the Python Library Reference).

displayhook(func)
Called by Python to display results in interactive sessions; assign sys.displayhook to a one-argument function to customize output.

__displayhook__
Original value of displayhook (for restores).

`exceptionhook(type, value, traceback)`

Called by Python to display exception details to stderr; assign `sys.exceptionhook` to a three-argument function to customize exception displays.

`__exceptionhook__`

Original value of `exceptionhook` (for restores).

`exc_info( )`

Returns tuple of three values describing the exception currently being handled: `(type, value, traceback)`. Specific to current thread. Subsumes `exc_type`, `exc_value`, and `exc_traceback` in Python 1.5 and later.

`exc_type`

Type of exception being handled (when an exception has been raised). Not thread-specific.

`exc_value`

Exception's parameter (second argument to `raise`). Not thread-specific.

`exc_traceback`

Exception's traceback object. Not thread-specific.

`exec_prefix`

Assigns a string giving the site-specific directory prefix where the platform-dependent Python files are installed; defaults to */usr/local* or a build-time argument. Used to locate shared library modules (in *<exec_prefix>/lib/ python<version>/lib-dynload*) and configuration files.

`executable`

String giving the file pathname of the Python interpreter program running the caller.

`exit([N])`

Exits from a Python process with status `N` (default 0) by raising `SystemExit` built-in exception (can be caught in a `try` statement and ignored). See also the `os._exit( )` function in "The os System Module," which exits immediately without exception processing (useful in child processes after an `os.fork( )`).

**exitfunc**

May assign a no-argument function to be called on exit.[*]

**getdefaultencoding( )**

Returns the name of the current default string encoding used by the Unicode implementation. New in 2.0.

**getrefcount(object)**

Returns object's current reference count value (+1 for the call's argument).

**getrecursionlimit( )**

Returns the maximum depth limit of the Python call stack; see also `setrecursionlimit`.

**_getframe([depth])**

Returns a frame object from the Python call stack (see the Python Library Reference).

**hexversion**

Python version number, encoded as a single integer (viewed best with the `hex` built-in function). Increases with each new release. New in 1.5.2.

**last_type**
**last_value**
**last_traceback**

Type, value, and traceback object of last uncaught exception (mostly for postmortem debugging).

**maxint**

Maximum positive value of plain integer on platform.

**modules**

Dictionary of modules already loaded; one `name:object` entry per module. Writable (e.g., `del sys.modules['name']` forces a module to be reloaded on next import).

---

[*] exitfunc is somewhat deprecated as of Release 2.0; use the atexit module instead.

path

> List of strings specifying module import search path. Initialized from PYTHONPATH shell variable and any installation-dependent defaults. Writable; e.g., `sys.path.append('C:\\dir')` adds a directory to the search path within a script.
>
> The first item, `path[0]`, is the directory containing the script that was used to invoke the Python interpreter. If the script directory is not available (e.g., if the interpreter is invoked interactively or if the script is read from standard input), `path[0]` is the empty string, which directs Python to search modules in the current working directory first. The script directory is inserted before the entries inserted from PYTHONPATH.

platform

> String identifying the system on which Python is running: e.g., `'sunos5'`, `'linux2'`, `'win32'`, `'PalmOS3'`. Useful for tests in platform-dependent code. Hint: `'win32'` means all current flavors of Windows, or test as `sys.platform[:3]=='win'`.

prefix

> Assigns a string giving the site-specific directory prefix, where platform-independent Python files are installed; defaults to */usr/local* or a build-time argument. Python library modules are installed in the directory *<prefix>/lib/python<version>*; platform-independent header files are stored in *<prefix>/include/python<version>*.

ps1

> String specifying primary prompt in interactive mode; defaults to >>> unless assigned.

ps2

> String specifying secondary prompt for compound statement continuations, in interactive mode; defaults to ... unless assigned.

`setcheckinterval(reps)`

> Call to set how often the interpreter checks for periodic tasks (e.g., thread switches, signal handlers) to reps. Measured in virtual machine instructions (default is 10). In general, a Python statement translates to multiple virtual machine instructions. Lower values maximize thread responsiveness but also maximize thread switch overhead.

`setdefaultencoding(name)`

> Call to set the current default string encoding used by the Unicode implementation. New in 2.0, and somewhat experimental.

`setprofile(func)`

> Call to set the system profile function to func: the profiler's "hook" (not run for each line). See the Python Library Reference for details.

`setrecursionlimit(depth)`

> Call to set maximum depth of the Python call stack to depth. This limit prevents infinite recursion from causing an overflow of the C stack and crashing Python.

`settrace(func)`

> Call to set the system trace function to func: the "hook" used by debuggers, etc. See the Python Library Reference for details.

`stdin`

> Standard input stream: a preopened file object. May be assigned to any object with read methods to reset input within a script (e.g., `sys.stdin=MyObj( )`). Used for interpreter input, including `raw_input( )` and `input( )` built-in function calls.

`stdout`

> Standard output stream: a preopened file object. May be assigned to any object with write methods to reset output

within a script (e.g., sys.stdout=open('log', 'a')). Used for some prompts and the print statement.

stderr
Standard error stream: a preopened file object. May be assigned to any object with write methods to reset stderr within a script (e.g., sys.stderr=wrappedsocket). Used for interpreter prompts/errors.

__stdin__
__stdout__
__stderr__
Original values of stdin, stderr, and stdout at program start (e.g., for restores).

tracebacklimit
Maximum number of traceback levels to print; defaults to 1,000.

version
String containing the version number of the Python interpreter.

version_info
Tuple containing five version identification components (see the Python Library Reference).

winver
Version number used to form registry keys on Windows platforms (see the Python Library Reference).

# The string Module and Methods

The string module defines constants and variables for processing string objects, above and beyond string type operations. See also string built-in type operations and string-related built-in functions in "Specific Built-in Types," and "The re Pattern-Matching Module."

## Module Functions Versus String Object Methods

As of Python 2.0, most functions in this module are also available as methods of string objects (see "Strings" in the earlier section "Specific Built-in Types" for more details and a list of all available string methods). A `string` module function call such as func(str, arg) is generally now also accessible as str.func(arg). Where appropriate, both call formats are listed.

Note that as of Python 2.2, much of the `string` module is available as object methods, but not all; constants and some module functions are still available only in the `string` module. Function entries with just one listed call signature are not available as string methods. Similarly, some string methods are not available in this module (see the string type in "Specific Built-in Types").

## Constants

digits
  The string '0123456789'.

hexdigits
  The string '0123456789abcdefABCDEF'.

letters
  Concatenation of the strings lowercase and uppercase.

lowercase
  Usually, the string 'abcdefghijklmnopqrstuvwxyz'.*

octdigits
  The string '01234567'.

printable
  Combination of digits, letters, punctuation, and whitespace.

---

\* lowercase, uppercase, whitespace, etc. depend on the current 8-bit locale; the examples shown are for 7-bit U.S. ASCII.

punctuation

> String of characters that are considered punctuation characters.

uppercase

> Usually, `'ABCDEFGHIJKLMNOPQRSTUVWXYZ'`.

whitespace

> String containing space, tab, linefeed, return, formfeed, and vertical tab.

## Functions and Methods

In all of the following, the result is a new string (since strings are mutable, they are never modified in-place). Whitespace means spaces, tabs, and end-of-line characters (everything in `string.whitespace`).

### Conversions

atof(s)

> Converts string s to floating-point. Like built-in `float( )` function.

atoi(s [, base])

> Converts string s to integer of given base (default is 10). Like built-in `int( )` function.

atol(s [, base])

> Converts string s to Python long integer (unlimited precision) of given base (default is 10). Like built-in `long( )` function.

### Searching

find(s, sub [, start [, end]])
s.find(sub, [, start [, end]])

> Returns offset of the first occurrence of string sub in s, between offsets start and end (which default to 0 and len(s), the entire string). Returns −1 if not found.

---

```
rfind(s, sub [, start [, end]])
s.rfind(sub, [, start [, end]])
```
> Like find, but scans from the end (right to left).

```
index(s, sub [, start [, end]])
s.index(sub [, start [, end]])
```
> Like find, but raises ValueError if not found instead of
> returning −1.

```
rindex(s, sub [, start [, end]])
s.rindex(sub [, start [, end]])
```
> Like rfind, but raises ValueError if not found instead of
> returning −1.

```
count(s, sub [, start [, end]])
s.count(sub [, start [, end]])
```
> Counts the number of nonoverlapping occurrences of sub
> in s, from offsets start to end (defaults: 0, len(s)).

## Splitting and joining

```
split(s [, sep [, maxsplit]])
s.split([sep [, maxsplit]])
```
> Returns a list of the words in string s. If sep is absent or
> None, splits string on whitespace characters. If sep, splits
> around sep occurrences. If maxsplit is nonzero, only
> splits that many times at the front of s (default 0).
> split('a*b','*') and 'a*b'.split('*') both yield
> ['a','b']. Use list(s) to convert a string to a list of
> characters (e.g., ['a','*','b']).

```
join(x [, sep])
sep.join(x)
```
> Concatenates a list or tuple of strings x into a single
> string. If no sep, add one space between each item. If sep,
> add it between items instead. sep can be '' (an empty
> string) to convert a list of characters to a string. Note the
> order for the string method equivalent: join(['a','b'],
> '*') and '*'.join(['a','b']) both yield 'a*b'. Also note
> that sep is not optional for method call formats.

```
```

```
replace(str, old, new [, maxsplit])
str.replace(old, new [, maxsplit])
```
Returns a copy of string str with all occurrences of substring old replaced by new. If maxsplit passed, the first maxsplit occurrences are replaced. Works like a combination of x=split(str,old) and join(x,new). old is a simple string; see the section "The re Pattern-Matching Module" for global search-and-replace tools based on pattern strings.

```
splitfields(s [, sep [, maxsplit]])
```
Same as split (retained for compatibility; earlier split took one argument).

```
joinfields(x [, sep])
```
Same as join (retained for compatibility; earlier join took one argument).

## Formatting

```
capitalize(word)
word.capitalize( )
```
Capitalizes the first character of string word.

```
capwords(s)
```
Splits string s into words using split, capitalizes each word using capitalize, and joins with join. A similar string method is s.title( ).

```
expandtabs(s [, tabsize])
s.expandtabs([tabsize])
```
Replaces tabs in string s with tabsize spaces (default is 8).

```
strip(s)
s.strip( )
```
Removes leading and trailing whitespace from string s.

```
lstrip(s)
s.lstrip( )
```
Removes leading whitespace from string s.

rstrip(s)
s.rstrip( )

    Removes trailing whitespace from string s.

swapcase(s)
s.swapcase( )

    Converts all lowercase to uppercase, and vice versa.

upper(s)
s.upper( )

    Converts all letters to uppercase.

lower(s)
s.lower( )

    Converts all letters to lowercase.

ljust(s, width)
s.ljust(width)

    Left-justifies string s in a field of the given width; pads with spaces on right. (Can also achieve with % string formatting expression.)

rjust(s, width)
s.rjust(width)

    Right-justifies string s in a field of the given width; pads with spaces on left. (Can also do with %.)

center(s, width)
s.center(width)

    Centers string s in a field of the given width; pads with spaces on left and right. (Can also do with %.)

zfill(s, width)

    Pads string s on left with zero digits to produce a string result of the desired width. (Can also do with %.)

maketrans(from, to)

    Returns translation table that maps each character in from into the character at the same position in to.

```
translate(s, table [, deletechars])
s.translate(table [, deletechars])
```
> Deletes all characters from string s that are in
> deletechars (if present), then translates the characters
> using table, a 256-character string giving the translation
> for each character value indexed by its ordinal.

# The os System Module

The os module is the primary operating system (OS) services
interface. It provides generic operating-system support and a
standard, platform-independent OS interface. The os module includes tools for environments, processes, files, shell
commands, and much more. It also includes a nested submodule, os.path, that provides a portable interface to directory processing tools.

Scripts that use os and os.path for systems programming are
generally portable across most Python platforms. However,
some os exports are not available on all platforms (e.g., fork
is available on Unix but not Windows). Because the portability of such calls changes over time, consult the Python
Library Reference for platform details.

## Administrative Tools

Following are some miscellaneous module-related exports:

error
> Known as both os.error and built-in OSError exception.
> Raised for os module–related errors. The accompanying
> value is a pair containing the numeric error code from
> errno and the corresponding string, as would be printed
> by the C function perror(). See the module errno in the
> Python Library Reference for names of the error codes
> defined by the underlying OS.

> When exceptions are classes, this exception carries two
> attributes: errno, the value of the C errno variable; and

strerror, the corresponding error message from strerror(). For exceptions that involve a file pathname (e.g., chdir(), unlink()), the exception instance also contains the attribute filename, the filename passed in.

name
> Name of OS-specific modules whose names are copied to the top level of os (e.g., "posix", "nt", "dos", "mac", "os2", "ce", "java"). See also sys.platform in "The sys Interpreter Module."

path
> Nested module for portable pathname-based utilities. Example: os.path.split is a platform-independent directory name tool that internally uses an appropriate platform-specific call.

## Portability Constants

This section describes tools for parsing and building directory and search path strings portably. They are automatically set to the appropriate value for the platform on which a script is running. See also "The os.path Module," later in the book, for additional portable filename-related tools.

curdir
> String used to represent current directory (e.g., "." for POSIX, ":" for Macintosh).

pardir
> String used to represent parent directory (e.g., ".." for POSIX, "::" for Macintosh).

sep
> String used to separate directories (e.g., "/" for Unix, "\" for Windows, or ":" for Macintosh).

altsep
> Alternative separator string or None (e.g., "/" for Windows).

pathsep

> Character used to separate search path components, as in the PATH and PYTHONPATH shell variable settings (e.g., ";" for Windows, ":" for Unix).

defpath

> Default search path used by os.exec*p* calls if there is no PATH setting in the shell.

linesep

> String used to terminate lines on current platform (e.g., "\n" for POSIX, "\r" for Mac OS, "\r\n" for MS-DOS and Windows).

## Shell Commands

These functions run programs in the underlying operating system:

system(cmd)

> Executes a command string cmd in a subshell process. Returns the exit status of the spawned process. Unlike popen, does not connect to cmd's standard streams via pipes. Hints: add an & at the end of cmd to run the command in the background on Unix (e.g., os.system('python main.py &')); use a DOS start command to launch programs easily on Windows (e.g., os.system('start file.html')).

startfile(filepathname)

> Starts a file with its associated application. Acts like double-clicking the file in Windows Explorer or giving the filename as an argument to a DOS start command (e.g., with os.system('start path')). The file is opened in the application with which its extension is associated; the call does not wait. Windows only, new in 2.0.

popen(cmd [, mode [, bufsize]])

> Opens a pipe to or from shell command string cmd, to send or capture data. Returns an open file object, which

may be used to either read from cmd's standard output stream stdout (mode 'r') or write to cmd's standard input stream stdin (mode 'w'). Example: dirlist = os.popen('ls -l *.py').read( ) gets the output of a Unix ls command.

cmd is any command string you can type at your system's console or shell prompt. mode may be 'r' or 'w' and defaults to 'r'. bufsize is the same as in the built-in open function. cmd runs independently; its exit status is returned by the resulting file object's close method, except that None is returned if exit status is 0 (no errors).

In the popen variants listed below, bufsize is the buffer size for the I/O pipes and mode is the string 'b' or 't', for binary or text transfer modes. mode defaults to 't'; 'b' is useful on Windows to force the file objects to be opened in binary mode and to suppress automatic linefeed conversions. The popen2 module exports similar calls, but return value order differs.

popen2(cmd [, bufsize [, mode]])
    Executes cmd as a subprocess and connects to both its standard input and output streams. Returns a tuple of two file objects: (child_stdin, child_stdout). New in 2.0.

popen3(cmd [, bufsize [, mode]])
    Executes cmd as a subprocess and connects to all three of its standard streams. Returns the file object's tuple (child_stdin, child_stdout, child_stderr). New in 2.0.

popen4(cmd [, bufsize [, mode]])
    Like popen3, but ties stdout and stderr to a single output pipe. Returns the file object's tuple: (child_stdin, child_stdout_and_stderr). New in 2.0.

## Environment Tools

These attributes export execution environment and context:

environ
    The shell environment variable dictionary. os.environ['USER'] is the value of variable USER in the shell

(equivalent to $USER in Unix and %USER% in DOS). Initialized on program startup. As of 1.5, changes made to os.environ by key assignment are exported outside Python using a call to C's putenv and are inherited by any processes that are later spawned in any way.

putenv(varname, value)

Sets the shell environment variable named varname to the string value. Affects subprocesses started with system, popen, spawnv, or fork and execv. Assignment to os.environ keys automatically calls putenv (but putenv calls don't update environ).

getcwd( )

Returns the current working directory name as a string.

chdir(path)

Changes the current working directory for this process to path, a directory name string. Future file operations are relative to the new current working directory.

strerror(code)

Returns an error message corresponding to code.

times( )

Returns a five-tuple containing elapsed CPU time information for the calling process, in floating-point seconds: (user-time, system-time, child-user-time, child-system-time, elapsed-real-time). Also see "The time Module" in "Other Built-in Modules."

tmpfile( )

Returns a new file object opened in update mode ('w+'). The file has no directory entries associated with it and will be automatically deleted once there are no file descriptors for the file.

umask(mask)

Sets the numeric umask to mask and returns the prior value.

uname( )
    Returns OS name tuple of strings: (*systemname*, *nodename*,
    *release*, *version*, *machine*). See also socket.gethostname()
    and socket.gethostbyaddr(socket.gethostname()).

confstr(name)
confstr_names
sysconf(name)
sysconf_names
    System configuration value access (see the Python
    Library Reference for details).

## File Descriptor Tools

The following functions process files by their descriptors (fd
is a file-descriptor integer). os module descriptor-based files
are meant for low-level file tasks and are not the same as
stdio file objects returned by the built-in open function
(though os.fdopen and the file object fileno method convert
between the two). File objects, not descriptors, should normally be used for most file processing.

close(fd)
    Closes file descriptor fd (not a file object).

dup(fd)
    Returns duplicate of file descriptor fd.

dup2(fd, fd2)
    Copies file descriptor fd to fd2 (close fd2 first if open).

fdopen(fd [, mode [, bufsize]])
    Returns a built-in file object (stdio) connected to file
    descriptor fd (an integer). mode and bufsize have the
    same meaning as in the built-in open function (see "Built-
    in Functions"). A conversion from descriptor-based files
    to file objects normally created by the built-in open func-
    tion. Hint: use fileobj.fileno to convert a file object to a
    descriptor.

fstat(fd)
   Returns status for file descriptor fd (like stat).

ftruncate(fd, length)
   Truncates the file corresponding to file descriptor fd, so
   that it is at most length bytes in size.

isatty(fd)
   Returns 1 if file descriptor fd is open and connected to a
   tty(-like) device.

lseek(fd, pos, how)
   Sets the current position of file descriptor fd to pos (for
   random access). how may be 0 to set the position relative
   to the start of the file, 1 to set it relative to the current
   position, or 2 to set it relative to the end.

open(filename, flags [, mode])
   Opens a file descriptor–based file and returns the file
   descriptor (an integer, not a stdio file object). Intended for
   low-level file tasks only; not the same as the built-in open
   function. mode defaults to 0777 (octal), and the current
   umask value is first masked out. flag is a bitmask: use "|"
   to combine flag constants defined in the os module (see
   Table 17).

pipe( )
   See the upcoming section "Process Control."

read(fd, n)
   Reads at most n bytes from file descriptor fd and returns
   those bytes as a string.

write(fd, str)
   Writes all bytes in string str to file descriptor fd.

fpathconf(fd, infoname)
fstatvfs(fd)
ttyname(fd)
openpty( )
   Consult the Python Library Reference or Unix manpages
   for details.

*Table 17. Or-able flags for os.open*

| O_APPEND | O_EXCL | O_RDONLY | O_TRUNC |
|----------|--------|----------|---------|
| O_BINARY | O_NDELAY | O_RDWR | O_WRONLY |
| O_CREAT | O_NOCTTY | O_RSYNC | |
| O_DSYNC | O_NONBLOCK | O_SYNC | |

## File Pathname Tools

The following functions process files by their pathnames (path is a string pathname of a file). See also the upcoming section "The os.path Module."

chdir(path)
getcwd( )
    See the earlier section "Environment Tools."

chmod(path, mode)
    Changes mode of file path to numeric mode.

chown(path, uid, gid)
    Changes owner/group IDs of path to numeric uid/gid.

link(srcpath, dstpath)
    Creates a hard link to file src, named dst.

listdir(path)
    Returns a list of names of all the entries in the directory path. A fast and portable alternative to the glob module and to running shell listing commands with os.popen.

lstat(path)
    Like stat, but does not follow symbolic links.

mkfifo(path [, mode])
    Creates a FIFO (a named pipe) named path with numeric mode mode (but does not open it). The default mode is 0666 (octal). The current umask value is first masked out from the mode. FIFOs are pipes that live in the filesystem and can be opened and processed like regular files. FIFOs exist until deleted.

`mkdir(path [, mode])`
>   Makes a directory called path, with the given mode. The default mode is 777, octal.

`makedirs(path [, mode])`
>   Recursive directory-creation function. Like `mkdir`, but makes all intermediate-level directories needed to contain the leaf directory. Throws an exception if the leaf directory already exists or cannot be created. mode defaults to 0777, octal. New in 1.5.2.

`readlink(path)`
>   Returns the path referenced by a symbolic link path.

`remove(path)`
`unlink(path)`
>   Removes (deletes) the file named path. `remove` is identical to `unlink`. See `rmdir` and `removedirs` for removing directories.

`removedirs(path)`
>   Recursive directory-removal function. Like `rmdir`, but if the leaf directory is successfully removed, directories corresponding to the rightmost path segments will be pruned away until either the whole path is consumed or an error is raised. Throws an exception if the leaf directory could not be removed. New in 1.5.2.

`rename(srcpath, dstpath)`
>   Renames (moves) file src to name dst.

`renames(oldpath, newpath)`
>   Recursive directory- or file-renaming function. Like rename, but creation of any intermediate directories needed to make the new pathname good is attempted first. After the rename, directories corresponding to the rightmost path segments of the old name will be pruned away using `removedirs`. New in 1.5.2.

`rmdir(path)`
>   Removes (deletes) a directory named path.

`stat(path)`
> Runs stat system call for `path`; returns a tuple of integers with low-level file information (whose items are defined and processed by tools in module `stat`).

`symlink(srcpath, dstpath)`
> Creates a symbolic link to file `src`, called `dst`.

`tempnam([dir [, prefix]])`
> Returns a unique pathname reasonable for creating a temporary file: an absolute path that names a potential directory entry in the directory `dir` (or in a common location for temporary files, if `dir` is either omitted or `None`). `prefix` provides a short prefix to the filename. No automatic creation or cleanup is provided.

`tmpnam( )`
> Returns a unique pathname reasonable for creating a temporary file: an absolute path that names a potential directory entry in a common location for temporary files. No automatic creation or cleanup provided.

`TMP_MAX`
> The maximum number of unique names that `tmpnam` generates before reusing names.

`utime(path, (atime, mtime))`
> Sets file `path` access and modification times.

`access(path, mode)`
`statvfs(path)`
`pathconf(path, infoname)`
`pathconf_names`
> Consult the Python Library Reference or Unix manpages for details.

## Process Control

The following functions are used to create and manage processes and programs. See also the earlier section "Shell Commands" for other ways to start programs and files.

---

abort( )
>   Sends a SIGABRT signal to the current process. On Unix,
>   the default behavior is to produce a core dump; on Win-
>   dows, the process immediately returns exit code 3.

execl(path, arg0, arg1,...)
>   Equivalent to execv(path, (arg0, arg1,...)).

execle(path, arg0, arg1,..., env)
>   Equivalent to execve(path, (arg0, arg1,...), env).

execlp(path, arg0, arg1,...)
>   Equivalent to execvp(path, (arg0, arg1,...)).

execve(path, args, env)
>   Like execv, but the env dictionary replaces the shell vari-
>   able environment. env must map strings to strings.

execvp(path, args)
>   Like execv(path, args), but duplicates the shell's actions
>   in searching for an executable file in a list of directories.
>   The directory list is obtained from os.environ['PATH'].

execvpe(path, args, env)
>   A cross between execve and execvp. The directory list is
>   obtained from os.environ['PATH'].

execv(path, args)
>   Executes the executable file path with the command-line
>   arguments args, replacing the current program in this
>   process (the Python interpreter). args may be a tuple or a
>   list of strings, and it starts with the executable's name by
>   convention (argv[0]). This function call never returns,
>   unless an error occurs while starting the new program.

_exit(n)
>   Exits the process immediately with status n, without per-
>   forming cleanup. Normally used only in a child process
>   after a fork; the standard way to exit is to call sys.
>   exit(n).

`fork( )`
> Spawns a child process (a virtual copy of the calling process, running in parallel); returns 0 in the child and the new child's process ID in the parent.

`getpid( )`
`getppid( )`
> Returns the process ID of the current (calling) process; `getppid( )` returns the parent process ID.

`getuid( )`
`geteuid( )`
> Returns the process's user ID; `geteuid` returns the effective user ID.

`kill(pid, sig)`
> Kills the process with ID `pid` by sending signal `sig`.

`mkfifo(path [, mode])`
> See the previous section, "File Pathname Tools" (files used for process synchronization).

`nice(increment)`
> Adds `increment` to process's "niceness" (i.e., lowers its CPU priority).

`pipe( )`
> Returns a tuple of file descriptors (`rfd`, `wfd`) for reading and writing a new anonymous (unnamed) pipe. Used for cross-process communication.

`plock(op)`
> Locks program segments into memory. `op` (defined in `<sys./lock.h>`) determines which segments are locked.

`spawnv(mode, path, args)`
> Executes program `path` in a new process, passing the arguments specified in `args` as a command line. `args` may be a list or a tuple. `mode` is a magic operational constant made from the following: names `P_WAIT`, `P_NOWAIT`, `P_NOWAITO`, `P_OVERLAY`, and `P_DETACH`. On Windows,

roughly equivalent to a fork+execv combination (fork is not yet available on Windows, though popen and system are). New in 1.5.2.

spawnve(mode, path, args, env)
> Like spawnv, but passes the contents of mapping env as the spawned program's shell environment. New in 1.5.2.

wait( )
> Waits for completion of a child process. Returns a tuple with child's ID and exit status.

waitpid(pid, options)
> Waits for child process with ID pid to complete. options is 0 for normal use, or os.WNOHANG to avoid hanging if no child status is available. If pid is 0, the request applies to any child in the process group of the current process. See also the process exit status-check functions documented in the Python Library Reference (e.g., WEXITSTATUS(status) to extract the exit code).

ctermid( )
tcgetpgrp(fd)
tcsetpgrp(fd, pg)
setgid(id)
setegid(id)
setpgrp( )
setpgid(pid, pgrp)
setreuid(ruid, euid)
setregid(rgid, egid)
setsid( )
setuid(id)
seteuid(id)
getgid( )
getpgrp( )
getegid( )
getgroups( )
forkpty( )
> Consult the Python Library Reference or Unix manpages for details.

# The os.path Module

Provides additional file directory pathname-related services and portability tool. This is a nested module: its names are nested in the os module within the submodule os.path (e.g., the exists function is obtained by importing os and using os.path.exists). Most functions in this module take an argument path, the string directory pathname of a file (e.g., "C:\dir1\spam.txt"). Directory paths are generally coded per the platform's conventions and are mapped to the current working directory if lacking a directory prefix. Hint: forward slashes usually work as directory separators on all platforms.

abspath(path)
> Returns a normalized absolute version of path. On most platforms, this is equivalent to normpath(join(os.getcwd(), path)). New in 1.5.2.

basename(path)
> Same as second half of pair returned by split(path).

commonprefix(list)
> Returns longest path prefix (character by character) that is a prefix of all paths in list.

dirname(path)
> Same as first half of pair returned by split(path).

exists(path)
> True if string path is the name of an existing file path.

expanduser(path)
> Returns string that is path with embedded "~" username expansion done.

expandvars(path)
> Returns string that is path with embedded "$" environment variables expanded.

getatime(path)
> Returns time of last access of path (seconds since the epoch). New in 1.5.2.

`getmtime(path)`
>  Returns time of last modification of path (seconds since the epoch). New in 1.5.2.

`getsize(path)`
>  Returns size, in bytes, of file path. New in 1.5.2.

`isabs(path)`
>  True if string path is an absolute path.

`isfile(path)`
>  True if string path is a regular file.

`isdir(path)`
>  True if string path is a directory.

`islink(path)`
>  True if string path is a symbolic link.

`ismount(path)`
>  True if string path is a mount point.

`join(path1 [, path2 [, ...]])`
>  Joins one or more path components intelligently (using platform-specific separator conventions between each part).

`normcase(path)`
>  Normalizes case of a pathname. Has no effect on Unix; on case-insensitive filesystems, converts to lowercase; on Windows, also converts "/" to "\".

`normpath(path)`
>  Normalizes a pathname. Collapses redundant separators and up-level references; on Windows, converts "/" to "\".

`samefile(path1, path2)`
>  Returns true if both pathname arguments refer to the same file or directory.

`sameopenfile(fp1, fp2)`
>  Returns true if both file objects refer to the same file.

samestat(stat1, stat2)
>    Returns true if both stat tuples refer to the same file.

split(path)
>    Splits path into (head, tail), where tail is the last path-
>    name component and head is everything leading up to
>    tail. Same as tuple (dirname(path), basename(path)).

splitdrive(path)
>    Splits path into a pair ('drive:', tail) (on Windows).

splitext(path)
>    Splits path into (root, ext), where the last component of
>    root contains no "." and ext is empty or starts with a ".".

walk(path, visitor, data)
>    Callback based directory tree walker. Performs a recursive
>    directory traversal. During the traversal, calls function
>    visitor with arguments (data, dirname, filesindir) for
>    each directory and subdirectory in the directory tree
>    rooted at path (including path itself if it is a directory). The
>    argument dirname names the visited directory; the argu-
>    ment filesindir is a list of all the filenames in directory
>    dirname; the argument data is the data object passed to
>    the walk call. visitor may modify filesindir to influence
>    the set of directories visited below dirname (e.g., delete
>    names to prune tree).

# The re Pattern-Matching Module

The re module is the standard regular expression–matching
interface (new in 1.5). Regular expression (RE) patterns are
specified as strings. This module must be imported.[*]

---

[*] A section on the prior regex module has been removed from the book;
regex is now considered deprecated, and all new development should use
the re module documented here for pattern matching.

## Module Functions

compile(pattern [, flags])

> Compile an RE pattern string into a regular expression object, for later matching. flags (combinable by bitwise | operator):

> I *or* IGNORECASE *or* (?i)

>> Case-insensitive matching.

> L *or* LOCALE *or* (?L)

>> Makes \w, \W, \b, \B, \s, \S, \d, and \D dependent on the current 8-bit locale (default is 7-bit U.S. ASCII).

> M *or* MULTILINE *or* (?m)

>> Matches to each new line, not whole string.

> S *or* DOTALL *or* (?s)

>> "." matches *all* characters, including newline.

> U *or* UNICODE *or* (?u)

>> Makes \w, \W, \b, \B, \s, \S, \d, and \D dependent on Unicode character properties (new in 2.0).

> X *or* VERBOSE *or* (?x)

>> Ignore whitespace in the pattern, outside character sets.

match(pattern, string [, flags])

> If zero or more characters at start of string match the pattern string, returns a corresponding MatchObject instance, or None if no match. flags as in compile.

search(pattern, string [, flags])

> Scans through string for a location matching pattern; returns a corresponding MatchObject instance, or None if no match. flags as in compile.

split(pattern, string [, maxsplit=0])

> Splits string by occurrences of pattern. If capturing ( ) are used in pattern, occurrences of patterns or subpatterns are also returned.

---

```
sub(pattern, repl, string [, count=0])
```
> Returns string obtained by replacing the (first count) left-most nonoverlapping occurrences of `pattern` (a string or an RE object) in `string` by `repl`. `repl` can be a string or a function called with a single MatchObject argument, which must return the replacement string. `repl` may also include sequence escapes \1, \2, etc. to use substrings that matched groups, or \0 for all.

```
subn(pattern, repl, string [, count=0])
```
> Same as sub, but returns a tuple: (`new-string`, `number-of-subs-made`).

```
findall(pattern, string)
```
> Returns a list of strings giving all nonoverlapping matches of pattern in string. If one or more groups are present in the pattern, returns a list of groups. New in 1.5.2.

```
escape(string)
```
> Returns `string` with all nonalphanumerics backslashed, such that it can be compiled as a string literal.

## Regular Expression Objects

RE objects are returned by the `re.compile` function and have the following attributes:[*]

```
flags
```
> The `flags` argument used when the RE object was compiled.

```
groupindex
```
> Dictionary of {group-name: group-number} in the pattern.

```
pattern
```
> The pattern string from which the RE object was compiled.

---

[*] In 1.6 and later, pattern and match objects are internal types, not Pattern-Object or MatchObject instances.

```
match(string [, pos [, endpos]])
search(string [, pos [, endpos]])
split(string [, maxsplit=0])
sub(repl, string [, count=0])
subn(repl, string [, count=0])
findall( string)
```
Same as earlier re module functions, but pattern is implied, and pos and endpos give start/end string indexes for the match.

## Match Objects

Match objects are returned by successful match and search operations, and have the following attributes. See the Python Library Reference for additional attributes omitted here.

pos, endpos
Values of pos and endpos passed to search or match.

re
RE object whose match or search produced this.

string
String passed to match or search.

group([g1, g2,...])
Returns substrings that were matched by parenthesized groups in the pattern. Accepts zero or more group numbers. If one argument, result is the substring that matched the group whose number is passed. If multiple arguments, result is a tuple with one matched substring per argument. If no arguments, returns entire matching substring. If any group number is 0, return value is entire matching string; else, returns string matching corresponding parenthesized group number in pattern (1...N, from left to right). Group number arguments may also be group names.

groups( )
Returns a tuple of all groups of the match; groups not participating in the match have a value of None.

---

start([group]), end([group])
> Indices of start and end of substring matched by group (or entire matched string, if no group). If match object M, M.string[M.start(g):M.end(g)]==M.group(g).

span([group])
> Returns the tuple (start(group), end(group)).

expand(template)
> Returns the string obtained by doing backslash substitution on the template string template, as done by the sub method. Escapes such as \n are converted to the appropriate characters, and numeric backreferences (\1, \2) and named backreferences (\g<1>, \g<name>) are replaced by the corresponding group.

## Pattern Syntax

Pattern strings are specified by concatenating forms (see Table 18) as well as by character class escapes (see Table 19). Python character escapes (e.g., \t for tab) may also appear. Pattern strings are matched against text strings, yielding a Boolean match result, as well as grouped substrings matched by subpatterns in parentheses.

### Example

```
>>> import re
>>> patt = re.compile('hello[ \t]*(.*)')
>>> mobj = patt.match('hello   world!')
>>> mobj.group(1)
'world!'
```

In Table 18, "C" is any character, "R" is any regular expression form in the left column of the table, and "m" and "n" are integers. Each form usually consumes as much of the string being matched as possible, except for the nongreedy forms (which consume as little as possible, as long as the entire pattern still matches the target string).

*Table 18. Regular expression pattern syntax*

| Form | Description |
| --- | --- |
| . | Matches any character (including newline if DOTALL flag is specified). |
| ^ | Matches start of string (of every line in MULTILINE mode). |
| $ | Matches end of string (of every line in MULTILINE mode). |
| C | Any nonspecial character matches itself. |
| R* | Zero or more occurrences of preceding regular expression R (as many as possible). |
| R+ | One or more occurrences of preceding regular expression R (as many as possible). |
| R? | Zero or one occurrence of preceding regular expression R. |
| R{m,n} | Matches from m to n repetitions of preceding regular expression R. |
| R*?, R+?, R??, R{m,n}? | Same as *, +, and ? but matches as few characters/times as possible; *nongreedy*. |
| [...] | Defines character set; e.g., [a-zA-Z] matches all letters (also see Table 19). |
| [^...] | Defines complemented character set: matches if character is not in set. |
| \ | Escapes special characters (e.g., *?+|( )) and introduces special sequences (see Table 19). Due to Python rules, write as \\ or r'\\'. |
| \\ | Matches a literal \; due to Python string rules, write as \\\\ in pattern, or r'\\'. |
| R\|R | Alternative: matches left or right R. |
| RR | Concatenation: matches both Rs. |
| (R) | Matches any RE inside ( ), and delimits a group (retains matched substring). |
| (?: R) | Same as (R) but doesn't delimit a group. |
| (?= R) | Look-ahead assertion: matches if R matches next, but doesn't consume any of the string (e.g., X (?=Y) matches X if followed by Y. |
| (?! R) | Negative look-ahead assertion: matches if R doesn't match next. Negative of (?=R). |

*Table 18. Regular expression pattern syntax (continued)*

| Form | Description |
|---|---|
| (?P<name> R) | Matches any RE inside ( ) and delimits a named group (e.g., r'(?P<id>[a-zA-Z_]\w*)' defines a group named id). |
| (?P=name) | Matches whatever text was matched by the earlier group named name. |
| (?<= R) | Positive look-behind assertion: matches if preceded by a match of fixed-width R. |
| (?<! R) | Negative look-behind assertion: matches if not preceded by a match of fixed-width R. |
| (?#...) | A comment; ignored. |
| (?letter) | letter is one of "i", "L", "m", "s", "x", or "u". Set flag (re.I, re.L, etc.) for entire RE. |

In Table 19, \b, \B, \d, \D, \s, \S, \w, and \W behave differently depending on flags: if LOCALE (?L) is used, they depend on the current 8-bit locale; if UNICODE (?u) is used, they depend on the Unicode character properties; if neither flag is used, they assume 7-bit U.S. ASCII. Tip: use raw strings (r'\n') to literalize backslashes in Table 19 class escapes.

*Table 19. Regular expression pattern special sequences*

| Sequence | Description |
|---|---|
| \num | Matches text of the group num (numbered from 1) |
| \A | Matches only at the start of the string |
| \b | Empty string at word boundaries |
| \B | Empty string not at word boundary |
| \d | Any decimal digit (like [0-9]) |
| \D | Any non-decimal digit character (like [^0-9]) |
| \s | Any whitespace character (like [ \t\n\r\f\v]) |
| \S | Any non-whitespace character (like [^ \t\n\r\f\v]) |
| \w | Any alphanumeric character |
| \W | Any non-alphanumeric character |
| \Z | Matches only at the end of the string |

# Object Persistence Modules

Three modules compose the object persistence interface:

anydbm
    Key-based string-only storage files.

pickle (and cPickle)
    Serializes an in-memory object to/from file streams.

shelve
    Key-based persistent object stores: pickles objects to/
    from anydbm files.

The shelve module implements persistent object stores.
shelve in turn uses the pickle module to convert (serialize) in-
memory Python objects to byte-stream strings and the anydbm
module to store serialized byte-stream strings in access-by-key
files. See also the "Python Portable SQL Database API" section later in the book (not part of the standard library).

## anydbm and shelve Interfaces

DBM is an access-by-key filesystem: strings are stored and
fetched by their string keys. The anydbm module selects the
keyed-access file implementation in your Python interpreter
and presents a dictionary-like API for scripts. A persistent
object shelve is used like a simple anydbm file, except that the
anydbm module is replaced by shelve, and the stored value can
be almost any kind of Python object (but keys are still strings).

```
import shelve
import anydbm
```
    Gets dbm, gbmd, bsddb... whatever is installed.

```
file = shelve.open('filename')
file = anydbm.open('filename', 'c')
```
    Creates a new or opens an existing dbm file.

```
file['key1'] = value
```
    Store: creates or changes the entry for 'key1'.

```
value = file['key2']
```
    Fetch: loads the value for the 'key2' entry.

```
count = len(file)
```
    Size: returns the number of entries stored.

```
index = file.keys()
```
    Index: fetches the stored keys list (can use in a for).

```
found = file.has_key('key3')
```
    Query: sees if there's an entry for 'key3'.

```
del file['key4']
```
    Delete: removes the entry for 'key4'.

```
file.close()
```
    Manual close; required to flush updates to disk for some underlying DBM interfaces.

### Notes

- dbm files and shelves work like dictionaries that must be opened before use; all mapping operations and some dictionary methods work.

- For dbm files and shelves, can also pass mode ('r', 'w', etc.) and protection (access-mode) parameters to open if desired (some DBM flavors require extra arguments).

## pickle Interface

The pickle interface converts nearly arbitrary in-memory Python objects to/from serialized byte streams. Byte streams can be directed to any file-like object that has the expected read/write methods. Unpickling re-creates the original in-memory object (with same value, but new identity).

See also the cPickle module (coded in C for speed enhancement and automatically used by shelve, if present), and the makefile method of socket objects (for shipping serialized objects over networks), both in the Python Library Reference.

```
P = pickle.Pickler(fileobject)
```
Makes a new pickler, for saving to an output file object.

```
P.dump(object)
```
Writes an object onto the pickler's file/stream.

```
pickle.dump(object, fileobject)
```
Combination of the previous two: pickles object onto file.

```
U = pickle.Unpickler(fileobject)
```
Makes unpickler, for loading from input file object.

```
object = U.load( )
```
Reads an object from the unpickler's file/stream.

```
object = pickle.load(fileobject)
```
Combination of the previous two: unpickles object from file.

```
string = pickle.dumps(object)
```
Returns pickled representation of object as a string.

```
object = pickle.loads(string)
```
Reads an object from a character string instead of a file.

### Notes

- `Pickler` and `Unpickler` are exported classes.
- `fileobject` is an open file object, or any object that implements file object attributes called by the interface. `Pickler` calls the file `write` method with a string argument. `Unpickler` calls the file `read` method with a byte-count and `readline` without arguments.

# Tkinter GUI Module and Tools

Tkinter is a portable graphical user interface (GUI) construction library shipped with Python as a standard library module. Tkinter provides an object-based interface to the open source Tk library and implements native look and feel for

Python-coded GUIs on Windows, X-Windows, and Mac OS. It is portable, simple to use, well-documented, widely used, mature, and well-supported.

## Tkinter Example

In Tkinter scripts, *widgets* are customizable classes (e.g., Button, Frame), *options* are keyword arguments (e.g., text="press"), and *composition* is object embedding, not pathnames (e.g., Label(Top,...)).

```
from Tkinter import *               # widgets, constants

def msg():                          # callback handler
    print 'hello stdout...'

top = Frame()                       # make a container
top.pack()
Label(top,  text="Hello world").pack(side=TOP)
widget = Button(top, text="press", command=msg)
widget.pack(side=BOTTOM)
top.mainloop()
```

## Tkinter Core Widgets

Table 20 lists the primary widget classes in the Tkinter module. These are true Python classes that may be subclassed and embedded in other objects. To create a screen device, make an instance of the corresponding class, configure it, and arrange it with one of the geometry manager interface methods (e.g., Button(text='hello').pack()).

*Table 20. Tkinter core widget classes*

| Widget class | Description |
| --- | --- |
| Label | Simple message area |
| Button | Simple labeled pushbutton widget |
| Frame | Container for attaching and arranging other widget objects |
| Toplevel, Tk | Top-level windows managed by the window manager |
| Message | Multiline text-display field (label) |

*Table 20. Tkinter core widget classes (continued)*

| Widget class | Description |
|---|---|
| Entry | Simple single-line text entry field |
| Checkbutton | Two-state button widget, used for multiple-choice selections |
| Radiobutton | Two-state button widget, used for single-choice selections |
| Scale | A slider widget with scalable positions |
| PhotoImage | Image object for placing full-color images on other widgets |
| BitmapImage | Image object for placing bitmap images on other widgets |
| Menu | Options associated with a Menubutton or top-level window |
| Menubutton | Button that opens a Menu of selectable options/submenus |
| Scrollbar | Bar for scrolling other widgets (e.g., Listbox, Canvas, Text) |
| Listbox | List of selection names |
| Text | Multiline text browse/edit widget, support for fonts, etc. |
| Canvas | Graphics drawing area: lines, circles, photos, text, etc. |
| OptionMenu | *Composite*: pull-down selection list |
| ScrolledText | *Composite*: Text with attached Scrollbar |
| Dialog | *Old*: common dialog maker (see new common dialog calls in the next section) |

## Common Dialog Calls

### Module tkMessageBox

```
showinfo(title=None, message=None, **options)
showwarning(title=None, message=None, **options)
showerror(title=None, message=None, **options)
askquestion(title=None, message=None, **options)
askokcancel(title=None, message=None, **options)
askyesno(title=None, message=None, **options)
askretrycancel(title=None, message=None, **options)
```

### Module tkSimpleDialog

```
askinteger(title, prompt, **kw)
askfloat(title, prompt, **kw)
askstring(title, prompt, **kw)
```

### Module tkColorChooser

```
askcolor(color = None, **options)
```

### Module tkFileDialog

```
class Open
class SaveAs
askopenfilename(**options)
asksaveasfilename(**options)
askopenfile(mode="r", **options)
asksaveasfile(mode="w", **options)
```

The common dialog call options are: defaultextension (added to filename if not explicitly given), filetypes (sequence of (label, pattern) tuples), initialdir (initial directory, remembered by classes), initialfile (initial file), parent (window in which to place the dialog box), title (dialog box title).

## Additional Tkinter Classes and Tools

Table 21 lists some commonly used Tkinter interfaces and tools beyond the core widget class and standard dialog set.

*Table 21. Additional Tkinter tools*

| Tool category | Available tools |
|---|---|
| Tkinter linked variable classes | StringVar, IntVar, DoubleVar, BooleanVar |
| Geometry management methods | pack, grid, place, plus configuration options |
| Scheduled callbacks | Widget after, wait, and update methods; file I/O callbacks |
| Other Tkinter tools | Clipboard access; bind/Event low-level event processing; widget config options; modal dialog box support |
| Tkinter extensions (Vaults of Parnassus site) | *PMW*: more widgets; *PIL*: images; *hackicon*: replace red Tk; *PythonWorks*: Tkinter GUI builder, etc. |

## Tcl/Tk-to-Python/Tkinter Mappings

Table 22 compares Python's Tkinter API to the base Tk
library as exposed by the Tcl language. In Python's Tkinter,
the Tk GUI interface differs from Tcl in the following ways:

*Creation*
> Widgets are created as class instance objects by calling a
> widget class.

*Masters (parents)*
> Parents are previously created objects, passed to widget
> class constructors.

*Widget options*
> Options are constructor or config keyword arguments,
> or indexed keys.

*Operations*
> Widget operations (actions) become Tkinter widget class
> object methods.

*Callbacks*
> Callback handlers are any callable object: function,
> method, lambda, etc.

*Extension*
> Widgets are extended using Python class inheritance
> mechanisms.

*Composition*
> Interfaces are constructed by attaching objects, not by
> concatenating names.

*Linked variables*
> Variables associated with widgets are Tkinter class
> objects with methods.

*Table 22. Tk-to-Tkinter mappings*

| Operation | Tcl/Tk | Python/Tkinter |
|---|---|---|
| Creation | `frame .panel` | `panel = Frame()` |
| Masters | `button .panel.quit` | `quit = Button(panel)` |

*Table 22. Tk-to-Tkinter mappings (continued)*

| Operation | Tcl/Tk | Python/Tkinter |
|---|---|---|
| Options | button .panel.go -fg black | go = Button(panel, fg='black') |
| Configure | .panel.go config -bg red | go.config(bg='red') go['bg'] = 'red' |
| Actions | .popup invoke | popup.invoke() |
| Packing | pack .panel -side left -fill x | panel.pack(side=LEFT, fill=X) |

# Internet Modules and Tools

This section summarizes Python's support for Internet scripting.

## Commonly Used Library Modules

Following are some of the more commonly used modules in the Python Internet modules set. This is just a representative sample; see the Python Library Reference for a more complete list.

socket
> Low-level network communications support (TCP/IP, UDP, etc.). Interfaces for sending and receiving data over BSD-style sockets: socket.socket() makes an object with socket call methods (e.g., object.bind()). Most protocol and server modules use this module internally.

select
> Interfaces to Unix and Windows select function. Waits for activity on one of N files or sockets. Commonly used to multiplex among multiple streams, or to implement timeouts. Only works for sockets on Windows, not files.

cgi
> Server-side CGI script support: cgi.FieldStorage parses the input stream; cgi.escape applies HTML escape conventions to output streams. To parse and access form

information: after a CGI script calls `form=cgi.FieldStorage()`, `form` is a dictionary-like object with one entry per form field (e.g., `form["name"].value` is form field name text).

`urllib, urllib2`

Fetches web pages and server script outputs from their Internet addresses (URLs): `urllib.urlopen(url)` returns file with read methods; also `urllib.urlretrieve(remote, local)`. Supports HTTP, FTP, gopher, local file URLs. Also has tools for escaping URL text: `urllib.quote_plus(str)` does URL escapes for text inserted into HTML output streams.

`ftplib`

FTP (file transfer) protocol modules. `ftplib` provides interfaces for Internet file transfers in Python programs. After `ftp=ftplib.FTP('sitename')`, `ftp` has methods for login, changing directories, fetching/storing files and listings, etc. Supports binary and text transfers; works on any machine with Python and an Internet connection.

`httplib, nntplib`

HTTP (web) and NNTP (news) protocol modules.

`poplib, imaplib, smtplib`

POP, IMAP (mail fetch), and SMTP (mail send) protocol modules.

`telnetlib, gopherlib`

Telnet and gopher protocol modules.

`htmllib, sgmllib, xmllib, xml package, HTMLParser`

Parses web page contents (HTML, SGML, and XML documents). `xml` package new in 2.0; `HTMLParser` new in 2.2.

`xmlrpclib`

XML-RPC remote method call protocol (new in 2.2).

`rfc822`

Parses email-style header lines.

---

xdrlib
  Encodes binary data portably (also see socket modules earlier in this list).

mhlib, mailbox
  Processes complex mail messages and mailboxes.

mimetools, mimify
  Handles MIME-style message bodies.

multifile
  Reads messages with multiple parts.

uu, binhex, base64, binascii, quopri
  Encodes and decodes binary (or other) data transmitted as text.

urlparse
  Parses URL string into components.

SocketServer
  Framework for general net servers.

BaseHTTPServer
  Basic HTTP server implementation.

SimpleHTTPServer, CGIHTTPServer
  Specific HTTP web server request handler modules.

rexec, Bastion
  Restricted code execution mode. Support for restricted (trusted/safe) execution of program code, especially useful for Internet-related applications.

Table 23 lists some of these modules by protocol type.

*Table 23. Selected Python Internet modules by protocol*

| Protocol | Common function | Port number | Python module |
| --- | --- | --- | --- |
| HTTP | Web pages | 80 | httplib, urllib, xmlrpclib |
| NNTP | Usenet news | 119 | nntplib |
| FTP data default | File transfers | 20 | ftplib, urllib |

Table 23. *Selected Python Internet modules by protocol (continued)*

| Protocol | Common function | Port number | Python module |
|---|---|---|---|
| FTP control | File transfers | 21 | `ftplib`, `urllib` |
| SMTP | Sending email | 25 | `smtplib` |
| POP3 | Fetching email | 110 | `poplib` |
| IMAP4 | Fetching email | 143 | `imaplib` |
| Telnet | Command lines | 23 | `telnetlib` |
| Gopher | Document transfers | 70 | `gopherlib`, `urllib` |

# Other Built-in Modules

This section documents a handful of additional built-in modules. See the Python Library Reference for details on all built-ins and the Vaults of Parnassus web site at *http://www.vex.net/ parnassus/* for third-party modules and tools.

## The math Module

The `math` module exports C standard math library tools for use in Python. Table 24 lists this module's exports; see the Python Library Reference for more details. Also see the `cmath` module for complex number tools and the *NumPy* system for advanced numeric work. `frexp` and `modf` return two-item tuples for a single argument.

Table 24. *math module exports*

| | | | |
|---|---|---|---|
| `pi` | `e` | `acos(x)` | `asin(x)` |
| `atan(x)` | `atan2(x,y)` | `ceil(x)` | `cos(x)` |
| `cosh(x)` | `exp(x)` | `fabs(x)` | `floor(x)` |
| `fmod(x,y)` | `frexp(x)` | `hypot(x,y)` | `ldexp(x,y)` |
| `log(x)` | `log10(x)` | `modf(x)` | `pow(x,y)` |
| `sin(x)` | `sinh(x)` | `sqrt(x)` | `tan(x)` |
| `tanh(x)` | | | |

## The time Module

Following is a partial list of time module exports. See the Python Library Reference for more details.

clock( )
> Returns the current CPU time as a floating-point number expressed in seconds (CPU time for process so far). Useful for benchmarking and timing code sections.

ctime(secs)
> Converts a time expressed in seconds since the epoch to a string representing local time (e g , ctime(time( ))). As of 2.1, the argument is optional and defaults to the current time if omitted.

time( )
> Returns a floating-point number representing UTC time in seconds since the epoch. On Unix, epoch is 1970.

sleep(secs)
> Suspends the process's execution for secs seconds. secs can be a float to represent fractions of seconds.

## Threading Modules

Threads are lightweight processes that share global memory (i.e., lexical scopes and interpreter internals) and all run in parallel within the same process. Python thread modules work portably across platforms.

thread
> Python's basic thread interface module. Tools to start, stop, and synchronize functions run in parallel. To spawn a thread: thread.start_new_thread(function, argstuple). Function start_new is a synonym for start_new_thread. To synchronize threads, use thread locks: lock=thread.allocate_lock( ); lock.acquire( ); *update-objects*; lock.release( ).

---

threading
>   Module threading builds upon thread, to provide thread-
>   ing-oriented classes: Thread, Condition, Semaphore, Lock,
>   etc. Subclass Thread to overload run action method.

Queue
>   A multiproducer, multiconsumer FIFO queue implemen-
>   tation, especially useful for threaded applications (see the
>   Python Library Reference).

# Major Python/C API Tools

These Python/C integration tools, available in the C library
generated when Python is compiled, are used to call Python
from C (embedding) and call C from Python (extending).
Note that the *SWIG* system (among others) can automate
much C extension module coding, and the *Distutils* tool is
useful for building extensions. See the Python/C API manual
for additional details and calls omitted here.

## General

#include "Python.h"
>   Main Python C include file; defines the Python/C API.

libpython2.2.a, python22.dll, *etc. (platform-dependent)*
>   Python C library, when linked-in in embedded mode.

PyObject*
>   Type signature of a generic Python object in a C program.

Py_Initialize( )
>   Called to initialize linked-in Python libraries in embed-
>   ded mode.

Py_InitModule(char *name, PyMethodDef methods_table[])
>   C extension module initialization call in extending
>   mode.

## Reference Counts

```
void Py_INCREF(PyObject *o)
void Py_XINCREF(PyObject *o)
```
> Increments the reference count for object o. Second format has no effect if o is NULL.

```
void Py_DECREF(PyObject *o)
void Py_XDECREF(PyObject *o)
```
> Decrements the reference count for object o. Second format has no effect if o is NULL.

## Data Translation

```
int PyArg_ParseTuple(PyObject *arg, char *format, ...);
```
> Converts a Python tuple to C values. arg must be a tuple (e.g., an argument list passed to a C function). format is a conversion format string, whose syntax is given in Table 25 and in the Python/C API manual (e.g., si specifies string and integer conversions). The remaining arguments are addresses of C variables of corresponding types. Returns 0 on errors.

```
int PyArg_Parse(PyObject *arg, char *format, ...);
```
> Converts a Python object to C values. Similar to PyArg_ParseTuple, but arg is not assumed to be a tuple (add parentheses in the format string to convert a true tuple). Useful for arbitrary result object conversions in embedded mode.

```
PyObject *Py_BuildValue(char *format, ...);
```
> Constructs a Python object from C values. format is similar to PyArg_ParseTuple, but arguments beyond format (which are input to the function, not output) are simple values, not pointers. Returns a new Python object, suitable for passing to the Python interpreter from a C function.

*Table 25. Common Python/C data-conversion codes*

| Format-string code | C data type | Python object type |
|---|---|---|
| s | char* | String (without embedded "\0") |
| s# | char*, int | String, length (any content) |
| i | int | Integer |
| l | long int | Integer |
| c | char | String |
| f | float | Floating-point |
| d | double | Floating-point |
| O | PyObject* | Raw (unconverted) object |
| O& | &converter, void* | Converted object (calls converter) |
| (*items*) | Targets or values | Nested tuple |
| [*items*] | Series of arguments/ values | List |
| {*items*} | Series of *key*, *value* arguments | Dictionary |

See also type-specific converters and constructors in the Python/C API manual (e.g., PyInt_FromLong creates a Python integer object from a C long and PyInt_AsLong converts a Python integer object to a C long value).

## Module Access

PyObject* PyImport_ImportModule(char *name)

Imports and returns a Python module. name may contain a dot to denote a package (directory) import. Returns a new reference to the imported module, or NULL on error.

PyObject* PyImport_ReloadModule(PyObject *m)

Reloads a module object. Similar to the built-in Python function reload(). Returns a new reference to the reloaded module, or NULL on failure.

```
PyObject* PyImport_AddModule(char *name)
```
Returns the named module object (a borrowed reference) in the modules dictionary if present; otherwise, creates a new object and inserts it there. If the module was not already loaded, returns an empty module object; use `PyImport_ImportModule` to truly import a module.

```
PyObject* PyImport_GetModuleDict( )
```
Returns a borrowed reference to the system module dictionary (`sys.modules`).

```
PyObject* PyModule_GetDict(PyObject *module)
```
Returns a borrowed reference to the module's namespace dictionary (`module.__dict__`).

## Exceptions

```
void PyErr_Print( )
```
Prints a standard traceback to `sys.stderr` and clears the error indicator.

```
PyObject* PyErr_Occurred( )
```
Tests whether the error indicator is set. If set, returns the exception type.

```
void PyErr_Clear( )
```
Clears the error indicator. If the error indicator is not set, there is no effect.

```
void PyErr_Fetch(PyObject **ptype, PyObject **pvalue,
  PyObject **ptraceback)
```
Retrieves the error indicator into three variables whose addresses are passed.

```
void PyErr_SetString(PyObject *type, char *message)
  void PyErr_SetObject(PyObject *type, PyObject *value)
```
Sets the error (exception) indicator. The second format accepts an arbitrary Python object for the exception value.

## Running Strings of Code

int Py_eval_input, Py_file_input, Py_single_input
  The start symbols from the Python grammar for isolated expressions, sequences of statements as read from a file, or a single statement, respectively.

int PyRun_SimpleString(char *command)
  Executes the Python source code in command in the module __main__. Returns 0 on success.

PyObject* PyRun_String(char *str, int start, PyObject *globals, PyObject *locals)
  Executes the Python source code from str in the scopes specified by the dictionaries globals and locals. start specifies the start symbol that should be used to parse the source code. Returns the result of executing the code as a Python object (new reference).

PyObject* Py_CompileString(char *str, char *filename, int start)
  Parses and compiles Python source code in str, returning the resulting code object. filename may appear in tracebacks or SyntaxError messages. Returns NULL on error.

PyObject *PyEval_EvalCode(PyCodeObject *co, PyObject *globals, PyObject *locals)
  Executes an already-compiled code object in the namespace dictionaries passed.

## Running Callable Objects

PyObject* PyEval_CallObject(PyObject *object, PyObject *args)
PyObject* PyObject_CallObject(PyObject *object, PyObject *args)
  Calls a callable Python object (e.g., a function or class), with arguments given by the tuple args. Returns the

result of the call on success (new reference). Use Py_
BuildValue("(si)", arg1, arg2)-type calls to build an
arguments tuple first. Like apply(object, args).

```
PyObject* PyEval_CallFunction(PyObject *object,
  char *format, ...)
PyObject* PyObject_CallFunction(PyObject *object,
  char *format, ...)
```
Calls a callable Python object, with a variable number of
C arguments. The C arguments are described by a Py_
BuildValue-style format string. Returns the call result.

```
PyObject* PyEval_CallMethod(PyObject *o, char *method,
  char *format, ...)
PyObject* PyObject_CallMethod(PyObject *o, char *method,
  char *format, ...)
```
Calls method of object o with a variable number of C
arguments. Returns call result. The C arguments are
described by a Py_BuildValue-style format string. Like o.
method(args).

## Running Files and Interactive Loops

```
int PyRun_AnyFile(FILE *fp, char *filename)
```
If fp refers to a file associated with an interactive device,
returns the value of PyRun_InteractiveLoop; otherwise,
runs PyRun_SimpleFile.

```
int PyRun_InteractiveLoop(FILE *fp, char *filename)
```
Reads and executes statements from a file associated
with an interactive device until EOF is reached. Prompts
use sys.ps1 and sys.ps2. Returns 0 at EOF.

```
int PyRun_SimpleFile(FILE *fp, char *filename)
```
Similar to PyRun_SimpleString, but the Python source
code is read from fp instead of from an in-memory string.
filename is the name of the file.

```
PyObject* PyRun_File(FILE *fp, char *filename,
  int start, PyObject *globals, PyObject *locals)
```
Similar to PyRun_String, but the Python source code is read from fp instead of from an in-memory string. filename is the name of the file.

```
int PyRun_InteractiveOne(FILE *fp, char *filename)
```
Reads and executes a single statement from a file associated with an interactive device. Returns 0 when the input is successfully executed.

## Object Access

```
PyObject *PyDict_New( )
```
Creates a new, empty dictionary object. Useful to serve as the namespace of embedded code not associated with a true module file.

```
int PyDict_SetItemString(PyObject *dict, char *key,
  PyObject *value)
```
Assigns a key in a dictionary (like dict[key]=value).

```
PyObject *PyDict_GetItemString(PyObject *dict,
  char *key)
```
Fetches a key's value from a dictionary (like dict[key]).

```
int PyObject_Print(PyObject *o, FILE *fp, int flags)
```
Prints an object o on file fp. Returns −1 on error.

```
int PyObject_HasAttrString(PyObject *o, char *attr_name)
int PyObject_HasAttr(PyObject *o, PyObject *attr_name)
```
Returns 1 if object o has the attribute attr_name; else, returns 0. Like hasattr(o, attr_name).

```
PyObject* PyObject_GetAttrString(PyObject *o,
  char *attr_name)
PyObject* PyObject_GetAttr(PyObject *o,
  PyObject *attr_name)
```
Retrieves an attribute named attr_name from object o. Returns new reference to the attribute value on success, or NULL on failure. Like o.attr_name.

```
int PyObject_SetAttrString(PyObject *o, char *attr_name,
  PyObject *v)
int PyObject_SetAttr(PyObject *o, PyObject *attr_name,
  PyObject *v)
```
Sets the value of the attribute named attr_name, for object o, to the value v. Returns −1 on failure. Like o. attr_name = v.

```
int PyObject_DelAttrString(PyObject *o, char *attr_name)
int PyObject_DelAttr(PyObject *o, PyObject *attr_name)
```
Deletes attribute named attr_name, for object o. Returns −1 on failure. Like del o.attr_name.

```
int PyObject_Cmp(PyObject *o1, PyObject *o2,
  int *result)
int PyObject_Compare(PyObject *o1, PyObject *o2)
```
Compares the values of objects o1 and o2 using a routine provided by o1, if one exists; otherwise, with a routine provided by o2. Second format returns the result of the comparison; first format returns in result. Like Python statement result = cmp(o1, o2).

```
PyObject* PyObject_Repr(PyObject *o)
PyObject* PyObject_Str(PyObject *o)
PyObject* PyObject_Unicode(PyObject *o)
```
Computes a string representation of object o. Like repr(o), str(o), and unistr(o).

```
int PyObject_IsInstance(PyObject *inst, PyObject *cls)
```
Returns 1 if inst is an instance of the class cls or a subclass of cls. If cls is a type object rather than a class object, returns 1 if inst is of type cls.

```
int PyObject_IsSubclass(PyObject *derived,
  PyObject *cls)
```
Returns 1 if the class derived is identical to or derived from the class cls; otherwise, returns 0.

```
int PyObject_IsTrue(PyObject *o)
```
Returns 1 if object o is considered to be true, and 0 otherwise. Like not not o.

```
PyObject* PyObject_Type(PyObject *o)
```
Returns a type object corresponding to the object type of object o. Like type(o).

```
int PyObject_Length(PyObject *o)
```
Returns length of object o. Like len(o).

```
PyObject* PyObject_GetItem(PyObject *o, PyObject *key)
```
Returns element of object o corresponding to the object key, or NULL on failure. Like o[key].

```
int PyObject_SetItem(PyObject *o, PyObject *key,
  PyObject *v)
```
Maps object component key to value v. Returns −1 on failure. Like o[key] = v.

```
int PyObject_DelItem(PyObject *o, PyObject *key)
```
Deletes mapping for key from object o. Like del o[key].

```
int PyObject_AsFileDescriptor(PyObject *o)
```
If o is an integer or long integer, returns its value; else, returns o.fileno().

See also type-specific access functions and macros (e.g., PyTuple_GET_ITEM), and abstract object category–specific functions in the Python/C API manual (e.g., PyList_Append performs list append operations, PyFile_AsFile returns a FILE* for a Python file object, and PySequence_GetSlice slices arbitrary sequences).

# Python Portable SQL Database API

Python's portable database API provides script portability between different vendor-specific SQL database packages. For each vendor, install the vendor-specific extension module, but write your scripts according to the portable database API. Your database scripts will largely continue working unchanged after migrating to a different underlying vendor package.

Note that database extension modules are not part of the Python standard library (you must fetch and install them separately). See the section "Object Persistence Modules" earlier in this book for simpler alternatives. Hint: the Python-based *gadly* SQL database system allows scripts to be proto-typed with the database API, before you install a vendor package.

## API Usage Example

```
from dcoracle import Connect
connobj = connect("user/password@system")
cursobj = connobj.cursor( )

value1, value2 = 'developer', 39
query = 'SELECT name, shoesize FROM empl WHERE job = ? AND
    age = ?'
cursobj.execute(query, (value1, value2))

results = cursobj.fetchall( )
for (name, size) in results:
    print name, size
```

## Module Interface

This and the following sections provide a *partial* list of exports; see the full API specification at *http://www.python.org* for details omitted here.

connect(parameters...)
> Constructor for connection objects; represents a connection to the database. Parameters are vendor-specific.

paramstyle
> String giving type of parameter marker formatting (e.g., "qmark" = "?" style).

Warning
> Exception raised for important warnings such as data truncations.

Error
> Exception that is the base class of all other error exceptions.

## Connection Objects

Connection objects respond to the following methods:

close( )
> Closes the connection now (rather than when __del__ is called).

commit( )
> Commits any pending transactions to the database.

rollback( )
> Rolls database back to the start of any pending transaction; closing a connection without committing the changes first will cause an implicit rollback.

cursor( )
> Returns a new cursor object using the connection.

## Cursor Objects

Cursor objects represent database cursors, used to manage the context of a fetch operation.

description
> Sequence of seven-item sequences; each contains information describing one result column: (*name*, *type_code*, *display_size*, *internal_size*, *precision*, *scale*, *null_ok*).

rowcount
> Specifies the number of rows that the last execute* produced (for DQL statements like select) or affected (for DML statements like update or insert).

callproc(procname [,parameters])
> Calls a stored database procedure with the given name. The sequence of parameters must contain one entry for each argument that the procedure expects; result is returned as a modified copy of the inputs.

`close()`
> Closes the cursor now (rather than when __del__ is called).

`execute(operation [,parameters])`
> Prepares and executes a database operation (query or command); parameters may be specified as list of tuples to insert multiple rows in a single operation (but executemany is preferred).

`executemany(operation, seq_of_parameters)`
> Prepares a database operation (query or command) and executes it against all parameter sequences or mappings in sequence seq_of_parameters. Similar to multiple execute calls.

`fetchone()`
> Fetches the next row of a query result set, returning a single sequence, or None when no more data is available.

`fetchmany([size=cursor.arraysize])`
> Fetches the next set of rows of a query result, returning a sequence of sequences (e.g., a list of tuples). An empty sequence is returned when no more rows are available.

`fetchall()`
> Fetches all (remaining) rows of a query result, returning them as a sequence of sequences (e.g., a list of tuples).

## Type Objects and Constructors

`Date(year,month,day)`
> Constructs an object holding a date value.

`Time(hour,minute,second)`
> Constructs an object holding a time value.

`None`
> SQL NULL values are represented by the Python None on input and output.

# Python Idioms and Hints

This section lists common Python coding tricks and general usage hints. Consult the Python Library Reference and Python Language Reference (*http://www.python.org/doc/*) for further information on topics mentioned here.

## Core Language Hints

- S[:] makes a top-level copy of any sequence object; copy.deepcopy(X) makes full copies.
- L[:0]=[X,Y,Z] inserts items at front of list L.
- L[len(L):]=[X,Y,Z] and L.extend([X,Y,Z]) insert items at end (like in-place "+").
- L.append(X) and X=L.pop( ) can be used to implement in-place stack operations.
- Use for key in D.keys( ): to iterate through dictionaries, or simply for key in D: in 2.2.
- Use K=D.keys( ); K.sort( ); for key in K: for ordered dictionary iteration.
- X=A or B or None assigns X to the first true object among A and B, or None if both are false (i.e., 0 or empty).
- X,Y = Y,X swaps the values of X and Y.
- red, green, blue = range(3) assigns integer series.
- Use try/finally statements to ensure that termination code is run.

## Environment Hints

- Use if __name__ == '__main__': to add self-test code at the bottom of module files; true only when file is run, not when it is imported as a library.
- To load file contents in a single expression, use bytes=open('filename').read( ).

- To iterate through text files, use `for line in file.xreadlines():` or simply `for line in file:` in 2.2.

- To make a file an executable script on Unix-like platforms, add a line like `#!/usr/bin/env python` or `#!/usr/local/bin/python` at the top and give the file executable permissions with a `chmod` command. On Windows, file icons may be clicked.

- Command-line arguments: `sys.argv`; shell environment: `os.environ`; standard streams: `sys.stdin/stdout/stderror`; filename expansion: `glob.glob("pattern")`, `os.listdir('.')`.

- To run shell commands from within Python scripts, use `os.system("cmdline")`, `output=os.popen("cmdline").read()`, or `os.popen2/3/4`, or `os.fork/exec`.

- The `dir([object])` function is useful for inspecting attribute namespaces; `print object.__doc__` often gives documentation.

- `print` and `raw_input()` use `sys.stdout/stdin` streams: assign to file-like objects to redirect I/O internally (or use new `print >> file, text` statement format).

## Usage Hints

- Use `from __future__ import` *featurename* to enable experimental language features that may break existing code.

- Intuition about performance in Python programs is usually wrong: always measure before optimizing or migrating to C. See the `profile` and `time` modules.

- See modules `unittest` (a.k.a. PyUnit) and `doctest` for unit-testing tools shipped with the Python standard library; `unittest` is a class framework; `doctest` scans documentation strings for tests and outputs.

- See the `pydoc` library module and script shipped with Python for extraction and display of documentation strings associated with modules, functions, classes, and methods.

- See the section "Warnings framework" in "Built-in Exceptions" and -W in "Command-Line Options" for details about turning off future-deprecation warnings emitted by the interpreter.

- See *Distutils*, *installer*, *py2exe*, *squeeze*, *freeze*, and other tools for Python program distribution options.

- See *installer* and *py2exe* for turning Python programs into *.exe* files for Windows.

- See *NumPy* for an extension that turns Python into a numeric/scientific programming tool, with vector objects, etc.

- See *SWIG* (and others) for a tool that can automatically generate glue code for using C and C++ libraries within Python scripts; see *pyinline* (and others) for alternatives.

- See *IDLE* for a development GUI shipped with Python, with syntax-coloring text editors, object browsers, debugging, etc.; see *PythonWin*, *Komodo*, *PythonWorks*, and others for additional IDE options.

- See *Emacs* help for tips on editing/running code in the Emacs text editor; type C-c? in python mode to access help. Also see Emacs OO-Browser support for Python. Other editors support Python as well (e.g., auto-indenting, coloring), including *VIM* and *IDLE*.

## Assorted Hints

- Important web sites:
  - *http://www.python.org*—Python home
  - *http://www.rmi.net/~lutz/*—for updates to this book
  - *http://www.oreilly.com*—the publisher's home
  - *http://www.vex.net/parnassus/*—third-party Python tool links

- You should always say "spam" and "eggs" instead of "foo" and "bar" in Python examples.

- Always look on the bright side of life.